TALES FROM THE

—————1962—————

NEW YORK METS

A Collection of the Greatest Stories Ever Told

JANET PASKIN

Sports Publishing L.L.C.
www.sportspublishingllc.com

Director of production: Susan M. Moyer
Project manager: Tracy Gaudreau
Developmental editor: Kipp Wilfong
Copy editors: Susan M. Moyer and Cynthia L. McNew
Dust jacket design: Christine Mohrbacher
Photo editor: Erin Linden-Levy
Front cover: Members of the 1962 New York Mets, including Jim Hickman,
Gil Hodges, Frank Thomas and Charlie Neal. ©Bettman/CORBIS

ISBN: 1-58261-768-6

Printed in the United States

Sports Publishing L.L.C.
www.sportspublishingllc.com

*To the 1962 Mets, who did more for baseball with
120 losses than most teams do with 120 wins.*

*And to Hilda and Seymour Weingarten,
the best baseball fans I know.*

CONTENTS

ACKNOWLEDGMENTS

When Sports Publishing's Mike Pearson asked me to write this book, I told him I could only agree if the members of the 1962 Mets I'd met while working on a story for *The Journal News* gave me their blessing. They did more than that. I am grateful to each of the players who took time to talk to me, especially Craig Anderson, Larry Foss, Solly Hemus, Jim Hickman, Jay Hook, Al Jackson, Sherman Jones, Rod Kanehl, Clem Labine, Ken Mackenzie, Felix Mantilla, Herb Moford, Frank Thomas, and Don Zimmer. Marv Throneberry's widow Dixie and Harry Chiti's widow Catherine were also helpful, as were Bob Mandt, who started as a Mets ticket salesman and worked his way up to vice president, and broadcasters Ralph Kiner and Bob Murphy.

The sportswriters who covered the Mets were as important as the players in making the 1962 season special. Maury Allen, Stan Isaacs, Steve Jacobson and Jack Lang are engaging storytellers and were generous with their time.

The staff at Baseball Hall of Fame research library was eminently resourceful and helpful.

I am indebted to Mike Pearson, who invited me to do this project, and to editor Kipp Wilfong, who made the entire experience a pleasure. The folks I work with and for at *The Journal News* were supportive throughout, especially Mark Leary, Susie Arth and Mike Rose. Special gratitude is due Jennifer Friedman, Kathryn Schulz, Craig Aaron, Laura Paskin, Barry Mendelsohn, Ron Paskin, and Nancy Hammer whom I am lucky to have both as readers and very much loved friends and family.

INTRODUCTION

The 2003 Detroit Tigers were losing. A lot. In June alone they lost all but five games out of 26, and by the time the All-Star break rolled around, they appeared poised to do the impossible: lose more games than the 1962 Mets.

So the sports editor at *The Journal News* asked me to call some of the '62 Mets and find out if they were watching the Tigers, hoping to shed the ignominious distinction of being the worst team in baseball's modern era once and for all.

Though most of the players haven't seen each other in years, their answers were as similar as if they'd rehearsed. Pitcher Jay Hook, who also happens to live in Michigan, put it most succinctly: "I wouldn't wish that on anybody."

Forty-plus years removed from the daily torture of losing game after game until 120 losses piled up, the '62 Mets have more than made their peace. Most were happy to share stories of the season, and through their tales, they revealed another reason they wanted to hold on to their record. Somehow, they said, the '62 Met team was uniquely equipped to deal with that kind of infamy; it was just one more thing that made them special.

It's true. The stars aligned when the '62 Mets were born, creating a team that lives in baseball's mythology. Remember:

The Mets were born of baseball's first expansion. In 1960, a whopping 16 teams played major league baseball. When the Mets and the Houston Colt .45s took the field in 1962, they completed the four-team expansion, but no one had any idea what to expect from a brand new team.

The Mets brought National League baseball back to New York. Not only had the Giants and the Dodgers moved West, but they'd done so in the cruelest way possible – in the same year. They left National League fans with nothing but bitterness. What were they supposed to do? Root for the Yankees?

The Mets had name players. They brought back old Dodgers, old Giants, but the operative word was "old." They might have been good when their teams left town in '57, but the intervening five years had not treated them kindly.

The Mets had Casey Stengel. He was a baseball genius and a reporter's dream. He called the press corps "my writers" and kept them awake—and entertained—until 4 a.m. He made covering a bad team fun for the sportswriters, who amplified that enthusiasm and translated it to the fans.

The Mets were terrible. But in true, bittersweet fashion, they were almost always competitive. They rarely got blown out, they sent the tying run to bat in more than 50 games, and still they managed to lose, lose, lose, in ways no one had ever seen before.

Finally, the Mets brought all of these things together in New York City, where America's brightest spotlight shines. Heck, the Mets got a tickertape parade down Broadway before they'd even played a game. How could Houston compete with that?

Truth be told, the Colts did just fine once both teams took the field, but that will never be the point of the '62 Mets' season. With general good humor and grace, the original Mets gave baseball some of its best stories, and those are the tales told here.

Chapter
1

THE BIRTH
OF THE METS

Team members of the 1962 New York Mets at the Polo Grounds. AP/WWP

The Very Beginning

New York had been without National League baseball for half a decade. Finally, on the horizon, a ray of hope: The New York Metropolitans.

The year was 1881. The New York Mutuals had been kicked out of the fledgling National League in 1876 for failing to complete the season, and New York was without baseball until '81, when the Metropolitans played 60 games against National League teams. Two years later, they joined the American Association, and in 1884, they won the pennant.

The team only survived three more years. The league accused owner Joseph Gordon of colluding with his brother-in-law, John Day, who had owned the National League's New York Giants since 1883. Gordon fought the league and ultimately bailed out with a quick sale to a Staten Island millionaire. The team went bankrupt, and the new owners and the league ended up in court. Ultimately the Metropolitans players were sold to an American Association team in Brooklyn and the franchise was dissolved.

The Angry Legions

By the 1950s, there was no greater New York City rivalry than Dodgers versus Giants, no better feud to boil the blood of fans. As if by grand conspiracy, the owners of both teams enraged their fans at the same moment. Following in the highly profitable footsteps of Lou Perini, who moved the Boston Braves to Milwaukee in 1953, and other owners who had padded their pocketbooks by moving their baseball teams, both Giants owner Horace Stoneham and Dodgers owner Walter O'Malley considered relocation. O'Malley made loud, public moves, starting in 1956 when he moved the Dodgers to New Jersey for a handful of "home" games. Stoneham held a more quiet, but by no means secret, debate and let it be known that several cities were bidding for the Giants. In August, the Giants announced that they would move to San Francisco. In October, the Dodgers announced they were moving to Los Angeles.

New Yorkers were irate. A crowd gathered at the Polo Grounds, chanting famously, "We want Stoneham ... with a rope around his neck!"

The Dodgers and Giants had been more than teams. They had provided identities, and now they were gone. (Of course, there was also an American League team in the Bronx, but 21 pennants in 35 years had turned the once-rebellious Yankees into the embodiment of the establishment. And National League fans wanted nothing to do with them.)

"I really didn't pay any attention to baseball from 1957 to 1961," recalled Bob Mandt, who grew up an avid Dodgers fan. "I was so angry with my team. I remember, my brother said to me a couple of times, 'Let's go down to Philadelphia and take in the Dodgers, they're gonna play the Phillies this Friday night.'

"I wouldn't cross the street to see them, I was so mad. I wasn't mad at baseball, but I didn't like the Yankees. I couldn't possibly root for the Yankees after hating them for so many years."

And a whole city of people—minus the Yankee fans—felt the same.

A Political Fix

New York City Mayor Robert Wagner was up for re-election in the fall of 1957, after both teams announced their move West. The last thing he wanted was thousands of National League fans heading to the polls to vote against the guy who let the Dodgers and Giants get away. He couldn't keep the teams in New York even though he had offered to build them a new stadium out in Queens, so he did the next best political thing: He appointed a committee and pledged his dedication to bringing National League baseball back to New York.

It turned out to be a pretty smart thing to do. New York got its team, and Wagner was still mayor when it happened.

Persuasion, Intimidation, Success

No one worked harder to return National League baseball to New York than attorney and sports fan William (Bill) Shea. A member of Mayor Wagner's committee that brought National League baseball back to New York, Shea used all of his lawyerly skills of persuasion and intimidation. They worked.

First Shea tried to woo the Cincinnati, Philadelphia, and Pittsburgh clubs to New York. He tried to convince the National League to expand. Neither worked, but Shea didn't give up. Shea teamed up with legendary general manager Branch Rickey, who, most famously, broke baseball's color barrier when he signed Jackie Robinson to the Dodgers in 1947.

In 1960, Shea and Rickey announced the formation of the Continental League, which they hoped would be baseball's third major league. The eight-team league would have franchises in Houston, Toronto, Denver, Minneapolis and—oh yes—New York. Three more teams would be added in cities to be named later.

It is unclear whether Shea and Rickey were really interested in owning and operating a third league or simply trying to squeeze the baseball establishment. Ford Frick, the commissioner of baseball, had already told Rickey that he thought a third league was a good idea, but it was his professional responsibility to never admit that publicly. So with financial backing from Jack Kent Cooke (who would later own basketball's Los Angeles Lakers and football's Washington Redskins), Lamar Hunt (who would later own football's Kansas City Chiefs), and millionaire baseball fan Joan Payson (who would later own ... well, you'll see), baseball had no choice but to take the third league seriously. Rather than face the competition, on October 17, 1960, the National League voted to add franchises in New York and Houston, starting in 1962. The proposal was brought before the owners by none other than Dodgers owner Walter O'Malley.

The eight-team American League wasn't interested in becoming baseball's smaller league and responded with an announcement of its own. The AL would expand for the 1961 season—less than six months away—and add franchises in Washington D.C. (the Senators were moving to Minneapolis, where they would be called the Twins) and Los Angeles. Movie star Gene Autry bought the new AL franchise in Los Angeles and named the team the Angels. Gen. Elwood Quesada, head of the Federal Aviation Association, led the new Washington ownership group.

As for the National League teams: Judge Roy Hofheinz bought a team for Houston, which was eventually named the Colt .45s. The New York franchise was awarded to the "Metropolitan Baseball Club, Inc.," as represented by Shea and business partner M. Donald Grant.

Certifiable

On March 6, 1961, the deal was done, and the Mets had it in writing. Warren C. Giles, the president of the National League, signed the following fiat:

"This is to certify that the Metropolitan Baseball Club, Inc. is a member of the National League of Professional Clubs and is entitled to all the rights and privileges granted by the constitution and rules of the League, including the franchise to operate a professional baseball club in the City of New York. This certificate is not transferable."

The Early Days and Deep Pockets of Mrs. Joan Payson

Joan Whitney was born in 1903, the daughter of Payne and Helen Hay Whitney, two very rich, sports-loving people. Payne Whitney had donated a gymnasium to Yale. Helen Hay Whitney helped found the Greentree Stables, whose horse Twenty Grand won the 1931 Kentucky Derby. Little Joan went to Miss Chapin's and Barnard for school and the Polo Grounds for baseball. Her mother was a passionate Giants fan, prone to the occasional shouting match in the stands. Joan Whitney, who later married Charles Shipman Payson and became known everafter as Mrs. Payson, told the *New York Times* that her mother used to throw hard-boiled eggs to her children at lunchtime. Babe Ruth came for lunch once and was dumbfounded to find that his hostess was pitching eggs at him. "He never would have believed she did it every day," Mrs. Payson said.

As an adult, Mrs. Payson invested—financially and emotionally—in baseball. She owned 10 percent of the Giants, and offered to buy out owner Stoneham when he began to consider moving the franchise. When the proposal to move the team to San Francisco was brought to a vote before the board of directors, Mrs. Payson cast the only dissenting vote.

So Mrs. Payson was the ideal person to approach when it came time to bring baseball back to New York. She paid $3 million dollars for 85 percent of the Continental League's stock. The baseball establishment informed her that she couldn't own stock in two teams in competing leagues, so she gave her shares of Giants stock to New York Hospital.

With expansion, the early ownership group included Pete Davis, of tennis' Davis Cup fame, and Dorothy Killiam, a Canadian heiress who was also a rabid Dodgers fan, but by the time it came to get the club off the ground, the Mets were Mrs. Payson's team.

Chapter
2

PUTTING A TEAM TOGETHER

Welcome Aboard, George Weiss

The New York Yankees instituted a mandatory retirement policy in 1960 that forced George Martin Weiss out of his job as the club's general manager. Though the Yankees considered him too old for the Bronx, they didn't want to see him in another front office either and retained him as a "paid adviser," with a condition that prohibited him from becoming the general manager of any other club.

That didn't stop Weiss. When New York's new National League baseball team inquired, he quickly agreed to sign on. Eight days after the National League officially awarded the franchise to New York, the Metropolitan Baseball Club, Inc., announced that Weiss would join the Mets.

Weiss: Cold but Competent

George Weiss had been in the front office of one baseball club or another for more than 40 years. He had started with the New Haven Colonials, then moved on to be the general manager of an International League franchise in Baltimore, then signed on with the Yankees. The Yankees won 19 pennants and 16 World Championships in the 29 years of Weiss's tenure. But he earned his reputation as one of the most difficult personalities in baseball.

"He was like a mortician," said Jack Lang, then a reporter for the *Long Island Press*. Lang covered the Dodgers until their move to Los Angeles and met Weiss in the following years, when Lang covered the Yankees. "He was a cold person. He didn't allow you to warm up to him. He had that haughtiness that the Yankees had maintained when they were winning all those pennants."

Even Weiss's wife thought he was a little on the chilly side. Hazel Weiss, as engaging a personality as her husband was cold, charmed reporters when word leaked that she had encouraged her husband to take the job with New York's new baseball team.

"I married him for better or for worse, but not for lunch," she said.

So George Weiss went back to work. The Yankees weren't thrilled, but there was little they could do. To make room for Weiss in a way that the team in the Bronx couldn't fight, M. Donald Grant gave up his own title as president and became the Chairman of the Board. Weiss came on as president, convincing the Yankees that the difference in title was real.

The new club had a head man in place, and Hazel Weiss had her husband out of the house.

The Giodgers—No, the Dogiants

It seemed New York had been waiting for its new baseball team forever. But what to call it?

That spring, the public was asked to vote for one of 10 names for the new team: Continentals, Burros, Mets, Skyliners, Skyscrapers, Bees, Rebels, NYBs, Avengers, or Jets.

The club received 2,563 pieces of mail from people who wanted to weigh in on the debate. In addition to the 10 proposed nicknames, the public offered 634 more options, including the wistful but awkward compromises of Metro-Dodgers and Metro-Giants. Mrs. Payson herself favored a name that wasn't on the list. She liked Meadowlarks, especially because the team's new stadium was going up in Flushing Meadows.

Of the public's suggestions, Mets was the top choice of 61 voters—more than any other name. It was also the second or third choice of some more voters and, given the many variations on "Mets" that had surfaced, generally liked by some 287 people.

Besides, everyone was calling the team "Mets" already. It echoed the club's corporate name; it was short enough to make headlines, literally; it alluded to the New York metropolitan area and would therefore appeal to both Dodgers and Giants refugees; and it had historical echoes, to the 1884 Metropolitans, who had, after all, won the pennant.

Things would not go so well for the Mets.

Charlie Hurth: Over Before He Got Started

Branch Rickey, the legendary Cardinals and Dodgers general manager, was originally slated to run New York's new team, from its first inception as a Continental League franchise. Rickey reportedly wanted $5 million to pay for ball players, which was a little too much even for made-of-money Mrs. Payson. So even though he had been so instrumental in bringing National League baseball back to New York, Rickey and the Mets parted ways. One writer eulogized Rickey's efforts this way: "The Continental League was Branch Rickey's final moment in the baseball sun."

Instead, the new club hired Rickey-protégé Charlie Hurth, who had been the president of the Southern Association. Hurth had signed a three-year contract with the Mets in 1960, when the team was still a part of the Continental League. His moment in the Mets' spotlight was short-lived. With Rickey out and George Weiss in, Hurth stayed on a little while longer, but it was clear that Weiss was going to do everything a general manager ought to do. By the time the season started, Weiss's assumption of those duties was complete. In the 1962 Mets yearbook, Grant, as Chairman of the Board, and Weiss, as President, are pictured on the second page. No general manager is listed at all.

K.C. = Casey

Charles Dillon Stengel was born July 30, 1890, in Kansas City, Missouri, and first nicknamed "Dutch," which he earned at Central High School. It seems impossible to imagine that he could have done anything else in life besides baseball, but he went from high school to dental school. He couldn't stay out of baseball though, and when he started playing ball, he earned his nickname: K.C., for Kansas City, which quickly became Casey.

Casey Stengel
DONALD UHRBROCK/TIME LIFE PICTURES/GETTY IMAGES

Casey, Where Are You When We Need You?

By the 1960s, Casey Stengel was a bona fide part of the New York baseball landscape. He had been a part of each of New York's baseball teams. He made four hits in his first four at-bats for the Dodgers in 1913 and stayed with the team through 1917. He joined the Giants from 1921-23 and during those years, met his wife, a silent movie actress named Edna Lawson, at the Polo Grounds. He managed the Dodgers from 1934-36. In 1937 the Dodgers paid him not to manage. New York's baseball writers threw him a going-away dinner, suggesting he was the only recently fired manager to be honored quite so nicely. He went on to manage the Boston Braves, with little success, and then disappeared into the minor leagues. He had better luck in the minors, but his qualifications were still in doubt when Stengel came back to manage the Yankees in 1949. Up to that point, none of his teams had ever finished in first place. The critics would live to eat their words.

Under Stengel's leadership, the Yankees won the pennant 10 times. Some first-place finishes seemed guaranteed, with Yogi Berra, Whitey Ford, Roger Maris and Mickey Mantle on the roster. But 10 in 12 years was more success than even Yankee fans dreamed of. By the time he was forced out by the same mandatory-retirement policy that left George Weiss out of a job—"My services are no longer required," he told reporters bluntly—Stengel had been to the World Series 14 times—four times as a player, ten times as a manager. With the Yankees, he had won 37 World Series games, more than any manager in history, and tied fellow Yankees manager Joe McCarthy for number of World Championships won, with seven.

Stengel had been around for so long, that when the Yankees pushed the 70-year-old out the door, it was generally assumed he was gone for good.

Stengel Signs On

Brooklyn Dodgers manager Leo Durocher was rumored to be in the running for the Mets' inaugural managerial job. A 72-year-old retiree beat him to the finish line.

Casey and Edna Stengel had retired from New York baseball life to Glendale, California, and he was working as the vice president of a bank when the Mets started making overtures. It took a long time to close the deal, and Stengel was reluctant to disclose a figure, but newspapers reported that he signed a one-year contract for around $85,000. The Mets had offered to retain him for four or five years. Stengel said one was enough to start, thanks.

Immediately, Stengel was back in business.

"You can say I'm happy to be going back to the Polar Grounds," he told reporters. He called the new club the Knickerbockers.

Stengelese

Casey Stengel was known for his trademark way of circumnavigating the English language, almost as much as for his success with the New York Yankees. And he was funny—sometimes because he tried to be. His way of confusing and obfuscating was so celebrated, it had its own name: Stengelese.

"Casey would be talking about a topic," pitcher Jay Hook explained. "And because he was always talking, he'd be thinking about the next subject he was going to talk about, and he'd jump to that subject. And he would have that line of thought going on, and he'd remember that he didn't finish the first subject, and he'd jump back to the first subject, so he'd have two or three thoughts going on in parallel."

Bob Mandt, who joined the Mets as a ticket salesman in 1962 and is now vice president of special projects, put it this way: "He was the kind of guy who would grab you at a cocktail party, and he'd get you in a corner, and he'd start talking. He'd be talking about something that happened that day in the ballgame, and then he'd be comparing it with something that happened in a ballgame 30 years earlier, and then he'd be comparing it with something that happened when he was with the Yankees, and then somehow, you'd be talking about Washington and the federal deficit, and then it would swing around to be talking about something that was in the paper, about a Mars probe, and it would just go on and on and on and on and the drinks would be flowing and you'd be wondering when he was going to get back to where he started. It was almost like a game he was playing with you and eventually—maybe, I think people exaggerate when they say three hours, but maybe an hour later—he would come back to exactly where he started. It was like all the pieces all of a sudden made sense that he had been talking about, even though individually, none of them seemed to add up."

More than a few people suggested that Stengel was a ham, putting on a show for the audience. And as soon as he signed on with the Mets, he was right back at it.

The Mets' Original Genius

"George Weiss had to be a brilliant man to take this team and name Casey Stengel as the manager," said original Met third-baseman Don Zimmer. "Because that was the specialty of this team, from Day One."

Casey Stengel was a hero in New York for his success with the Yankees. He was revered as a great baseball mind. But more importantly, for the purposes of a team that would go on to lose so many games, Stengel gave the sportswriters and broadcasters something to write about, and in so doing, he gave the fans something to talk about.

From a professional standpoint, Stengel was more fun for the sportswriters than he was for the broadcasters. Everything on television is very carefully timed, and whenever Stengel went on television, it was always a trick to get him off the air.

"Casey was such a nonstop talker," said Mets broadcaster Bob Murphy. "I remember Lindsey Nelson was getting ready to do an interview with Casey. And Lindsey said, 'When it's time to close the interview out, I'll wink at you.' And Casey said, 'It's a good idea!'

"So they talked for about ten minutes, Lindsey winked at Casey. Casey winked back at him."

The Fine Pickings of the Expansion Draft

When baseball voted for expansion, the American League hurried to get its two new teams ready for the start of the 1961 season. The league immediately froze existing

American League rosters, which made some decent players eligible for the expansion draft. Even though the expansion Angels finished eighth and the new Senators tied for ninth, that was still more success than the National League owners were willing to risk.

So they rigged the draft. Each club had to make 15 players available, seven of whom had been on the club's 25-man roster as of August 31. The Philadelphia Phillies lost 107 games in 1961, and later claimed, according to Ralph Kiner's biography, that they had only done so badly because they had shipped all their talent to the minors to protect them from the expansion draft. The remaining available players were not exactly pennant material.

"There were some pretty good names on that list [of available players], but overall, they had ball players who could probably do one thing, where before they'd be able to do all three—hit, run and throw," Mets coach Solly Hemus said. "But those were the only players available, [the Mets] didn't have a scouting system at that point, so that's what they had to select from and do their best."

Houston general manager Paul Richards was irate.

"Richards thought it was a joke, the names they were putting in," Jack Lang said. "He thought it was like picking a bunch of ballplayers up off the street. The night before the draft in Cincinnati, he was furious with the names on the list. He couldn't pull out because his owners wouldn't let him. They had already made a financial commitment to play. He didn't like the cards he was dealt but he was going to have to play them whether he liked them or not."

Richards wasn't quiet about his feelings and complained so loudly that the National League officials silenced him. According to the *New York Times*, his last official comment on the draft was, "I never would have complained, if I'd realized so many fine players would be available."

Most Players/One Trade

Paul Richards and George Weiss were joined in the perpetuity of baseball trivia long before the 1962 expansion. In 1954, when Weiss was general manager of the Yankees and Richards was general manager of the Orioles, the two put together an 18-player trade. The deal took two weeks and is on record as the most players to be involved in one trade in baseball history.

The Name Player Strategy

There were two approaches to the rather slim pickings available in the expansion draft: either take underripe talent, players who might mature after a season or two in the majors, or select veterans a little past their peak.

Houston chose the former tactic. The Colt .45s didn't need any name-brand players. Houston had been strictly a minor league town and people there were excited just to have a major league team.

They'd never go for that in New York, George Weiss figured. He had to play to seasoned baseball fans, people who had loved—and lost—World Series teams. He needed players people would recognize. The problem was, any player a Giants or Dodgers fan would recognize was five years older than he had been the last time they'd seen him.

"They were all over their peak, by a wide margin," 1962 Mets outfielder John DeMerit said. "They wanted to put a bunch of names on the field that might put some people in the seats."

In fact, 922,530 people would pay to see the Mets, significantly more than saw the Giants in their last year at the Polo Grounds. The Colts, incidentally, wouldn't do too badly either, drawing 924,456 fans.

George Weiss, left, with Casey Stengel
DONALD UHRBROCK/TIME LIFE PICTURES/GETTY IMAGES

C h a p t e r
3

MEET THE METS

Draft Day

On October 10, 1961, the Mets recorded their first loss, in a coin toss to Houston to open the National League expansion draft. The Mets chose 22 players: 16 for $75,000 each, two more for $50,000 each, and finally, four premium picks for $125,000 each. The Colt .45s selected Eddie Bressoud with their first pick.

The First Choice

With their first pick, the Mets selected Hobie Landrith, 31, a catcher from San Fransisco. The Mets must have drafted Landrith for his fielding. He'd averaged in the low to middling .200's over 11 years in the major leagues, with a propensity for singles.

Stengel explained, "You've got to have a catcher, otherwise you're going to have a lot of passed balls."

Craig Anderson: A New Team, a New Wife

The Mets selected Craig Anderson, a 23-year-old right-hander from St. Louis, for $75,000. Nineteen-sixty-one was a middling year for Anderson, who hadn't started a game for the Cardinals and pitched fewer than 40 innings in relief. He had met a girl, though.

"I met Judy in St. Louis on Labor Day in 1961, and we had a whirlwind courtship," Anderson recalled. "Four days before we got married, they held the draft. I didn't know whether I was going to be selected or not. But the Cardinals put seven players in the pool. And of the seven players, the oldest was Bob Willis, who I think was 30 at the time. Most of the teams in the National League put up were much older guys. So almost all the Cardinal players were selected. Solly Hemus who had been my manager was now a coach for the Mets, and I think that was one of the reasons I got to play for the Mets."

Roger Craig: The Ace

The Mets paid the Dodgers $75,000 for Roger Craig, a 31-year-old right-handed pitcher. Craig had been a Dodger since his debut in 1955 and gone to the World Series three times. He'd won 12 games in 1956 and 11 in 1959, but by 1961, he was best cut out for relief. The Mets were counting on him to be the ace of the staff, and though reporter Steve Jacobson called him "princely," it is possible Craig knew he was in trouble. Union Oil had done a series of promotional, "Meet the Dodgers"-type booklets. On the front of Craig's, beneath his picture, was a quote: "Good infielders help."

A Righty and a Lefty

For $75,000 each, the Mets drafted Ray Daviault, a 27-year-old right-handed pitcher from the Giants, who hadn't played a major league season, and Al Jackson, a 26-year-old southpaw from Pittsburgh, who had only slightly more experience. He had pitched in 11 major league games in his two years (1959 and 1961) in the majors, and his career record was 1-0. What's more, he had been hoping to play for Houston, where he was living at the time.

"You know, I was from Texas," said Jackson. "So I thought it would be nice to stay close to home."

Two More Catchers

The Mets drafted two catchers, each for $75,000: Chris Cannizzaro, a 23-year-old from the St. Louis farm system, who had missed most of 1961 after an appendectomy, and Clarence (Choo Choo) Coleman, 25, from Philadelphia, who had played his first major-league baseball games in 1961 —34 of them, in which he had 47 at-bats and hit .128.

Ed Bouchee: Talented Player, Tumultuous Past

Ed Bouchee, a 28-year-old first baseman, fetched Chicago $75,000 from the Mets. Bouchee had been the National League Rookie of the Year in 1957 with Philadelphia with 17 home runs, 76 RBI and a .293 batting average. The next year was not as good. The six-foot first baseman showed up at spring training 35 pounds overweight and played half as many games for the Phillies; he also battled an indecent exposure charge in his hometown of Spokane, Washington, after he invited two girls, ages six and 10, into his car and showed them pornography. After he returned to baseball, he never reached or passed the success of his rookie year.

Ed Bouchee
DONALD UHRBROCK/TIME LIFE PICTURES/GETTY IMAGES

Elio Chacon: Fresh off the World Series

Elio Chacon had limited major league experience, but he had caught the nation's—and the Mets'—attention during the 1961 World Series. The 25-year-old infielder was the son of the great Cuban ballplayer Pelayo Chacon and had spent his first four years playing professional baseball in Havana, but in '61 joined the Cincinnati Reds for 61 games, including the championship.

In the second game of the World Series with the Yankees, Chacon won the hearts of Reds fans when, with two out in the fifth inning, he raced home on a passed ball to give the Reds a 3-2 lead. Cincinnati stretched the margin to a 6-2 win, their only one of the series. The incident was fresh enough in the minds of Yankees-haters; the Mets drafted Chacon in the $75,000 round.

Sammy Drake: Small Results, Big Gamble

Sammy Drake, a 27-year-old infielder from Chicago, had played in the major leagues for two years, amassing 20 at-bats and just one hit. That didn't stop the Mets. They took him for $75,000.

Gil Hodges: Home at Last

Gill Hodges, a 37-year-old first baseman, was one of the bigger names in the draft, at least as far as New York was concerned. Like Roger Craig, he'd been a Dodger his whole career. In 15 seasons Hodges had hit 361 home runs, more than any other right-handed batter in National League history, and he'd played in the World Series seven times and the six All-Star games.

He was a Dodgers fan favorite. According the Mets yearbook, on a hot summer Sunday in 1953, the Rev. Thomas Redmond announced to his Brooklyn parish that it was too hot for a sermon and he sent them home with the following instructions: "Observe the Ten Commandments, and pray for Gil Hodges to come out of his slump."

The mail came pouring in. Dodgers fans from all over the city sent letters, rosary beads, mezuzahs, rabbits feet, four-leaf clovers, and horseshoes. Hodges went on to hit .302, and the Dodgers won the pennant.

Hodges still commanded this kind of adoration when the Mets drafted him for $75,000, but his body was failing. He had consistent knee trouble, and his playing time, and productivity, had dropped precipitously in the previous two seasons.

Gus Bell: A Player's Player

Gus Bell was an everyday player. In fact, the 33-year-old outfielder had played almost every day since 1950, his rookie year with Pittsburgh. In 1955, he played in all 154 ballgames for Cincinnati. He hit .308 that year, but never since, and the Mets took him from the Reds for $75,000.

Joe Christopher: Speed, but What Else?

The Mets paid $75,000 for Joe Christopher, a 26-year-old outfielder, from Pittsburgh. Christopher was famous for being the first major-leaguer from the Virgin Islands, and his playing career was distinguished primarily by his speed. Christopher scored two runs in the 1960 World Series as a pinch-runner without having an at-bat. The Mets hoped he was fast enough to cover the Polo Grounds' vast outfield, but expectations for his offensive contribution were more modest. Even the Mets' yearbook suggested his statistics could use a boost: "Christopher is not a long ball hitter," his biography read, "but there is evidence that if he is able to play regularly, his speed will enable him to show a commendable batting average."

John DeMerit: Leaving Home

John DeMerit was a 25-year-old outfielder and one of Milwaukee's first bonus babies. He had signed a $100,000 contract in 1957 as a University of Wisconsin junior but hadn't played a full season with the Braves. Until the Mets drafted him for $75,000, he had never played for a team outside of his home state.

"I wasn't overly surprised [to be drafted]," he said. "Like anything else, it's a shakeup, you start over. All the people you knew are somewhere else. It was a change, and I was hoping it was a change for the better. In retrospect, I wish I had gone with Houston."

Inconsistent Smith

Bobby Gene Smith, a 27-year-old outfielder, from Philadelphia, also garnered $75,000 from the Mets. Smith was mostly a singles hitter, and his record suggests he was plagued by inconsistency in his five years in the major leagues, first with St. Louis, then Philadelphia.

Two Grateful Pitchers

For $50,000, the Mets took two more: Sherman (Roadblock) Jones, 26, a right-handed reliever, from Cincinnati, and Jim Hickman, a 24-year-old outfielder, from St. Louis.

A fastball pitcher, Jones had earned his nickname pitching for a minor-league team in Tacoma, Washington. He closed out both ends of a double-header, and a local sportswriter wrote that when Jones took the mound, "the road to home was blocked." His major-league record was less distinctive: a few saves, a few wins, a middling ERA. Playing in New York, he hoped, would change all that.

"This was the beginning of what I hoped would be my career," he said. "And there's no better place to start a career than New York. The Reds told me [I had been drafted]. My name was on the list. I wouldn't say I was sorry. I thought it was an opportunity, really."

Hickman had never played in a major league game, though during the 1961 season with Portland, in the Pacific Coast League, scouts were impressed with his speed. He was a generally consistent hitter in the minors, with 103 home runs in six seasons, but no one knew what he would do against major league pitching.

Hickman found out he was drafted from television reports.

"I was happy to go," he said. "I was just glad to get in the big leagues. I didn't know then—you're just in the expansion draft, you're glad to be there, and you just wait and see what happens."

The Reds Lose Jay Hook

Jay Hook, a 24-year-old right-handed pitcher with the pennant-winning Cincinnati Reds, was listening to the radio when he found out the Mets had made him a $125,000 premium pick in the final rounds of the expansion draft.

"My wife and I were at the World Series," Hook said. "And the kids had gone back, and we were driving home from the World Series, and I heard that I'd been traded or bought on the radio. I was surprised. I didn't know what to expect."

The Mets didn't know what to expect either. Hook had missed most of the 1961 season with the mumps. In five starts, he'd won one, lost three, and amassed an ERA of 7.76.

"I wasn't really on the team," Hook said. "I was back on in August, and I really wasn't effective at all. So the Reds put me up as a draft choice, and I think they probably figured nobody would pick me, because I hadn't really done much in 1961, because I'd been sick. But the Mets did pick me. And actually, after the Mets drafted me, they wanted me to go take a physical—or I'd had a physical and the report said that my white blood count was still real high. So they insisted I go to a doctor and be treated that fall.

"It was mixed emotions. The Reds had a pretty good team. At that time, when I saw who the other [Mets] picks were, I thought, we're going to have a pretty decent club. Because there were a lot of guys there who were known players. If you're going to play baseball, New York is a great place to play."

Jay Hook
BRACE PHOTO

The First Robert Miller

The Mets paid the St. Louis Cardinals $125,000 for Robert L. Miller, a 22-year-old right-handed pitcher. He had been an usher at Craig Anderson's wedding just days before the draft. He was mostly a middle reliever, with a 4.24 ERA over 35 games.

Robert L. Miller
BRACE PHOTO

Don Zimmer Gets His Wish

Don Zimmer, a 30-year-old infielder, wanted out of the Chicago Cubs. He said as much on the radio, mocking the team's experiment with the College of Coaches, and got his wish when the Mets drafted him for $125,000.

Zimmer had debuted with the Dodgers in 1954, played with the team in the 1955 World Series and then through the move to Los Angeles, where he played until 1959. The Dodgers won the World Series that year, too, but Zimmer hit .165 and was traded to Chicago. He hovered around .250 and the Cubs finished seventh in the next two years.

"That's the year, 1961, that we didn't have a manager," Zimmer said. "Mr. Wrigley had come up with the idea of having nine or 10 revolving coaches. No manager. One guy takes it for 10 days, the next guy for two weeks, and to me it was a circus. It was a joke. And the last day of the season, in '61, Lou Boudreau was in the radio booth, and he asked me if I would go on the pre-game show. He said, 'What do you think about the nine revolving coaches?' And I told him.

"'I don't want to get any of my teammates involved in this,' I told him. 'You're asking me, I'm going to answer it my way. I don't know how many years I have left in this game, but this is absolutely ridiculous.'

"When I made those comments, I knew I was going to rub some people wrong, but I didn't care, because if I was going to play another couple years I'd prefer to go elsewhere, where you had a manager. When I was done, I went down by the dugout, Charlie Grimm was still in the radio booth. He said, 'I heard your radio thing, and you said it the way you wanted to say it, and I respect you for that, but I'm quite sure you'll be gone.' And that didn't bother me at all.

"It turned out, they withdrew one guy [from the list of players eligible for the expansion draft] and put me on it, and I went to the Mets when the expansion happened. I didn't want to stay in Chicago. I thought it was a bad situation. Can you imagine, nine different managers in nine weeks? What fun would that be? And I just let it be known, I said, I'd rather go elsewhere and play the way it's supposed to be."

Short-Lived Lee Walls

The Mets paid $125,000 for Lee Walls, and the Phillies' 29-year-old outfielder never even put on a Met uniform. He had hit .280 in 1961, with eight home runs, and New York traded Walls and $100,000 to the Dodgers for Charlie Neal, who would turn 31 before the 1962 season began. In total, the 30-year-old Neal cost the team $225,000, and some wondered if he was worth it. The infielder had started with the Dodgers in 1956 and starred in the World Series three years later. Over the last two summers, the Dodgers had not done so well, and Neal's waning production made him a scapegoat for the team's troubles. But he had been a Dodger and certainly qualified as one of Weiss's "name players," so the Mets hoped for a return to form.

Trader George

George Weiss started trading right away. His team had just handed over $375,000, or 20 percent of its budget, to

Chicago, a team which had finished ninth in 1961, 29 games out of first place. It was clear the team needed more help than that.

Eight of the 25 players drafted were traded away; others finished their season in the minor leagues. Ken MacKenzie, a pitcher in Milwaukee's minor-league system who was signed shortly after the draft, called the team's roster, "a revolving door. Players didn't move around that much in those days," he said. "But it seemed there was a lot of coming and going with the Mets."

Almost as soon as the draft was over, Weiss was busy pushing people through that door. Weiss continued to pull together players, and as many big names as he could get his hands on.

On October 11, Weiss bought MacKenzie, a 27-year-old left-handed pitcher, and Johnny Antonelli, from the Braves. Antonelli opted out of the deal, but MacKenzie was still young and looking for a place to settle in. He had had two 14-win seasons with Atlanta, of the Southern League, then won six in each of the last three years with Louisville.

Frank Thomas

On Nov. 28, 1961, Weiss signed Frank Thomas. The 32-year-old outfielder had been an All-Star three times, but he was a little on the prickly side, which earned him his nickname, "Big Donkey." There was no quarrelling with his bat, though, and he always hit well in the Polo Grounds. Thomas played with Pittsburgh from 1951-58, and in the Giants' last four years at the Polo Grounds. Thomas ranked second only to Stan Musial in home runs hit there by visiting players.

Thomas went from Pittsburgh to Cincinnati to Chicago and finally to Milwaukee, where he spent the better part of the '61 season. He fit right in with Hank Aaron and Joe Adcock, and by the time he joined the Mets, he'd hit 223 career home runs.

Going to the Mets, Thomas said, "really didn't make much difference to me. The only thing that bothered me was when [Milwaukee general manager] John McHale, before I signed my contract, said that I was going to be their left fielder come 1962. And he lied to me. Because I said, 'If you have intentions of trading me, I'd appreciate it if you'd let me deal with the club I'm going to, rather than signing a contract.' I said, 'If you'd give me the opportunity to play regular again, you can give me a contract and I'll sign it.'"

Trusting McHale, Thomas signed his contract with Milwaukee. McHale sold him to New York, for cash and a player to be named later.

Richie Ashburn

In early December, George Weiss added another big-name bat to the lineup: Richie Ashburn. The outfielder came to the Mets with quite a resume. He'd been one of Philadelphia's Whiz Kids, when the Phillies won the pennant in 1950—the first time in 35 years. He'd been to the all-star game three times. He was fast, too, and sometimes called "The Cornhusker Express," because he was from Nebraska, or "Put Put," after Ted Williams said, "That put put has twin motors on his pants."

Philadelphia traded Ashburn to Chicago before the 1960 season, and by the time he got to the Mets, Ashburn was something of an elder statesman, with 2,455 hits at the beginning of the season.

Now All We Need Is ... Everything

While Weiss signed ballplayers, a frantic group was working furiously behind the scenes to put the team together. The Mets top brass opened offices in Canada House, on Fifth Avenue, but the basement of the Hotel Martinique, a fleabag on 32nd Street and Eighth Avenue, housed the everyday business staff. The space had been a store for Howard Clothes, which became one of the Mets' first sponsors and turned its space over to the team. To hear Bob Mandt tell it, the room shook every time a subway went by, and the rumbling set off the alarmed vault several times a day. There were, Mandt said, "perverts in the men's room" and the ladies' wasn't so nice either, as the women on the business staff eventually told the management that they absolutely needed better facilities. The Mets rented a premium apartment on the third floor, so that everyone would have a clean place to use the bathroom.

A long marble staircase stretched down to the offices from the lobby. At the top of the staircase, a sign read, "Met ticket office," with an arrow pointing down. The sign gave rise to one of the most often-told early Mets stories, and one that speaks to how little New Yorkers knew about their new baseball team.

A man came down the stairs, walked into the office, and asked for tickets to Rigoletto. "First-base side or third-base side?" came the response.

The Logo and the Beer

By the end of November, the Mets were able to check off two more items on their list of things to do. They had a logo, and they had beer.

On November 13, the Mets announced the Liebmann Brewing Co., which made Rheingold beer, would sponsor the radio and television broadcasts for five years. The company paid approximately $1 million a year for the privilege.

Three days later, the Mets unveiled their new logo. The team had run an open contest, which an artist named Ray Gatto won. The logo was a baseball, trimmed in Giant orange with orange stitching, and provided the backdrop for a Dodger blue silhouette of the New York City skyline. A white bridge stretched across the front, beneath an orange script "Mets."

Dodger Blue, Giants Orange

In the middle of February, Don Zimmer got a call at his home in St. Petersburg, Florida.

"The Met uniforms just got here," he was told. "Can you come down here and put one on?"

"Here" was Miller Huggins field, the Yankees' old spring training camp, in St. Petersburg. The Yankees were moving their spring training to Ft. Lauderdale, and the Mets swooped down to grab the old facility.

So Zimmer went down to the field, his six-year-old son Tom in tow. They mugged for the cameras.

"The picture, I have on my mantle," Zimmer said. "I'm in a Mets uniform and my son is on my shoulders."

But the carefully chosen orange and blue uniform didn't make Zimmer feel like Dodgers days were back again.

"I never paid too much attention to colors," he said. "Numbers don't mean much to me, either."

Maybe it would have meant more if he'd gotten his old Dodger number, 23, back as well. Zimmer wore number 17, which had been his number in Chicago.

Raising Consciousness

Only a smattering of fans knew who—or what—the Mets were. In the office at the Martinique, ticket salesmen were left to make cold calls. They started with the phone book.

"A couple of the guys who were working there had worked for the Yankees," Mandt said. "So we knew basically what the categories were for people who might want to buy a season box. We took the Manhattan yellow pages and the Queens yellow pages and Bronx and Brooklyn, and we took those categories out. We just ripped the book apart, and we gave one guy freight companies, and one guy got brokerage firms. Whatever the Yankees had had the most success with, we knew. Airlines, too, at that time. Everybody got on cold calls. You were just calling people up and saying, 'It's the Mets.' 'Who's the Mets?' Nobody knows."

Good Seats Still Available

The tickets arrived in the middle of March and later than expected. They came by rail, and all at once, in big crates. Now that the Mets actually had something tangible to sell, they moved Mandt and a co-worker into ticket booths at Penn Station and Grand Central Station. They hoped to catch commuters, but Mandt's station, at least, was tucked away in the waiting room. He sat behind a long counter, in front of a Mets banner, and waited the day away while passengers slept or read. Unfortunately, they didn't know what the Mets were either.

"Even though there was a great big Mets logo, people were so harried, looking for their train, that they didn't see it," he said. "They'd say, 'What time is the next train to Babylon?' Or, 'Can I get two tickets to Montauk?' And I would explain to them, this is the Mets."

Slowly, the public caught on. The Mets sold around 1,800 season ticket packages, at $215 each, plus $10 to join the private "Diamond Club," a cinder-block hospitality suite at the Polo Grounds. Regular tickets cost $3.50, $2.50, and $1.30. On Ladies Days, women paid 50 cents.

Stengel during a welcoming parade in New York City, April 12, 1962.
AP/WWP

Chapter
4

WHERE TO PLAY

So New, It Wasn't Done Yet

Mayor Robert Wagner promised a new National League baseball stadium as far back as 1956, as incentive to keep the Dodgers or Giants in New York. When the National League expanded, Wagner extended the same offer to the Mets, who enthusiastically accepted.

It felt like baseball would expand again before ground was actually broken. Gov. Nelson Rockefeller authorized legislation to build the 55,000-seat arena in early spring of 1961, and construction was scheduled to start by mid-May, so the Mets could play their first home game there less than a year later.

In June 1961, the Metropolitan Baseball Club, Inc., was still negotiating the lease with the Parks Department. Once the lease was finalized, it still had to be approved by the Board of Estimate, which held the city's purse strings. The Board, however, was reluctant to commit municipal money before the new ball club was officially granted a charter, as there was no other projected tenant, or use, for the new stadium.

Suffice it to say that promises, projections and crossed-fingers aside, the Mets were already looking around for another place to play, and temporary residency at the Polo Grounds was secured by the time workers broke ground in Flushing Meadows at the end of October 1961.

The Polo Grounds

The horseshoe-shaped stadium had hosted enough historic sporting events to spawn its own trivia game. They played football there, too—Army, Navy, Fordham, NYU, the professional club, the Titans. After Notre Dame beat Army 13-7 there, on Oct. 18, 1924, Grantland Rice dubbed the Notre Dame backfield "the Four Horsemen of the Apocalypse." The Fordham Wall stood there; Red Grange galloped the field; Tim Mara gave New York professional football and they played in the Polo Grounds. The same stadium had hosted Jack Dempsey fights and, more recently, Floyd Patterson's heavyweight championship bout against Ingemar Johansson.

As for baseball: The Giants won 10 pennants in 20 years in the Polo Grounds, from 1904 to 1924. The Giants won 26 straight games at home in the summer of 1916. The Yankees played there from 1913-1922; in '21 and '22, the Yankees played the Giants in the World Series, all the games were home games, and the Giants won both years. (Yankee Stadium opened in 1923, and finally the Yankees beat the Giants for the World Championship.) In more recent Polo Grounds history, Bobby Thomson hit the 1951 "shot heard round the world," a ninth-inning homer off the Dodgers' Ralph Branca to win a three-game playoff and the pennant for the Giants. And in 1954, Willie Mays made "The Catch" at the end of an impossibly long run to right center field to snag Vic Wertz's line drive over his shoulder, in a 10-inning game the Giants went on to win.

Short Porches

Baseball in Polo Grounds was peculiar (and unique and beloved) for the field's obscure dimensions. Because the diamond sat in the base of a rectangular football field, home plate was a stone's throw to the foul poles—257 feet to left, 279 to right—but center field stretched 483 feet to the bleachers. Before the Mets moved in, no one had homered to centerfield besides the Milwaukee Braves' Joe Adcock in 1953. Babe Ruth had hit two to centerfield in the Polo Grounds in 1921, but the bleachers had been reconfigured since then, so Adcock stood alone in the stadium's record books.

It was a long way to hit a ball and a long way to chase one, but it seemed even farther to walk out there after a loss. The clubhouses at the Polo Grounds were nestled in by the centerfield bleachers, a total baseball anomaly, even 40 years ago.

"The players didn't enter the field through the dugout, which was between home and first, they would enter the field coming down the steps of the clubhouse and walking the long walk to the dugout," said *Newsday* columnist Stan Isaacs. "And if a pitcher was knocked out of the game, well, sometimes he went to the dugout, but most of the time he'd leave the pitchers mound, and go out to the clubhouse about four hundred feet away."

If an outfielder did get all the way out to centerfield to run down a ball during the course of a game, he had to watch his step. The stairs to the clubhouses along the centerfield bleachers were in play, as were both bullpens.

"You could watch everything right in front of you," pitcher Craig Anderson said, of the view from the Mets' bullpen in right centerfield. "If a ball came our way, we had to get out of the way."

On Its Last Legs

For all its quirky charm, the truth was, the Polo Grounds was falling apart.

"It was sort of like some of the players I played with," Jim Hickman said. "I had read about it and heard about it all those years, and I knew the '51 series was there. I'd seen pictures of it and everything. I was really in awe of it. I was just tickled to death to be given the opportunity to play there for a couple of years before they tore it down."

The seats were narrow, and some of the views were obstructed. The roofs over the clubhouses leaked.

After one particularly rough night, Mets first-baseman Marv Throneberry was sitting in front of his locker, with a steady drip, drip, drip of water hitting him in the head.

"I deserve this," Throneberry said aloud.

"Yes," replied Richie Ashburn, who lockered next to Throneberry. "Yes, you do."

A Quick Face Lift

The Mets' new stadium would not be ready for any part of the 1962 season, but it was meant to be done for the 1963 home opener. So it didn't make any sense for the Mets to sink money into remodeling the Polo Grounds.

Except for rebuilding the playing field, the repairs were entirely cosmetic. The club spent $300,000 to repaint parts of the stadium, to spruce up telephone booths, bathrooms and ticket booths, to install a $50,000 electronic scoreboard. New air-conditioners were put in the dugouts, a new television studio was built, new flags were run up the poles. The playing field was reconstructed entirely with topsoil and new grass – a Merion blue, imported from Long Island at 12 cents per foot.

In the Radio Booth

The team was drafted, tickets printed, stadium painted. Even the broadcasters were getting used to their new studio.

George Weiss had hired Ralph Kiner, Lindsey Nelson, and Bob Murphy as the Mets' new broadcasters. Nelson came to the job from a long career as a football announcer. Murphy had been a broadcaster for the Baltimore Orioles, but couldn't resist the lure of New York. After a Hall of Fame baseball career with the Pirates, Kiner had been a general manager in the Pacific Coast League, then stepped into the booth for a year with the White Sox. He was scheduled to return to the White Sox when the Mets approached him.

"The Mets were starting up, and I was doing the broadcast of the Bing Crosby tournament in Pebble Beach when they called me," Kiner said. "And Lindsey was working that tournament and I asked him, 'What do you think I should do?' He said, 'I think you should come with the Mets.'"

What's important, Nelson told Kiner, is that they would be starting fresh; they wouldn't be replacing anyone or living up to expectations established by prior announcers. Nelson had already agreed to join the Mets, and so had Murphy. They were looking for a ball player. Kiner was the last to sign on.

The first time the trio met in New York, Weiss summoned them to a meeting in his office. It didn't take long.

"You know what to do," he told them. "Go and do it."

"[Nelson and Murphy] were great," Kiner said. There was no pressure or anything at all. I'd worked one year, so I knew what the broadcasting was like. They were very easy and made the job very simple. The fans were fantastic. And the television was in its infancy, so we sort of grew up with television."

Chapter 5

SPRING TRAINING

Early Expectations

T he outlook for the Mets was not rosy, exactly, but a generalized optimism hung around the new club in the winter. No one knew what the Mets would look like until spring training had officially begun.

"Over the winter, there was some feeling that Stengel, because he had been so successful with the Yankees that he could work some magic," *Newsday* columnist Stan Isaacs said. "Once spring training started, I think most of us pretty much began to be aware that this was going to be a pretty bad team."

Welcome to Florida

Quite a bit of the Mets' New York organization had come over from the Yankees with Weiss and Stengel, and nothing was different in Florida. The Yankees had moved from their longtime home in St. Petersburg to a field nearer to cosmopolitan Fort Lauderdale, leaving Miller Huggins field vacant. The Mets didn't care that it was named for the manager who led the Yankees to six pennants and three World Series Championships. Maybe they thought it would bring them luck. (Superstitious or not, eventually the name was changed to Al Lang field, after the former Pirates owner who had gone on to become the mayor of St. Petersburg.)

George Weiss also installed himself at the Yankees' old spring headquarters, the Soreno Hotel. It was an odd choice, given that the Yankees had left St. Petersburg at least in part because it was hard to run an integrated team in a segregated town. While St. Petersburg was progressing slowly, the Soreno had never allowed black players to stay there.

Players with children were allowed to find their own housing, but most of the team, along with Casey Stengel, lived at the Colonial Inn. The hotel draped a banner across the front door that read, "Home of the New York Mets and Casey Stengel." A sign at the front desk proudly proclaimed, "Stengelese spoken here."

Jackson Finds Prejudice

Al Jackson, the Texan pitcher, drove out to spring training with Bennie Daniels. They had been teammates together in Pittsburgh in 1959 and stayed friends. Daniels was on his way to spring training with the Senators, and the two decided to carpool to Florida.

When Al Jackson arrived at the Colonial Inn, he was greeted by the vestiges of segregated Florida. Jackson went inside, checked in, and went up to his room. He was tired after the long drive, and hungry too. He thought about

Al Jackson
BRACE PHOTO

going down to the hotel's restaurant, but fatigue won out. Jackson was pondering what to order from the room service menu when his phone rang. It was the front desk. Would Jackson please come down to see them?

Jackson had no idea what they wanted, but he obliged. The hotel manager called him into an office and explained that there were some places that Jackson, being black, couldn't go. The restaurant, for one. The pool, for another.

"I was shocked," Jackson said. "But I took it with a grain of salt."

Walking out of the office, Jackson ran into Lou Niss, the team's traveling secretary. Niss introduced himself to Jackson, who knew Niss by name but not by sight.

"He said, 'Is everything all right?'" Jackson recalled. "So I told him what happened. And he flew off the handle."

It simply would not do, Niss angrily told the hotel, to divide his team on account of hotel prejudice or policy. They worked out a solution: the hotel gave the entire team a separate room off the dining room for breakfast and dinner.

"I guess if the blacks couldn't go in the restaurant, the white guys couldn't go in either," Jackson said.

Communication Breakdown

No one had heard from Elio Chacon all winter. The Mets had sent the shortstop, for whom they'd paid $75,000 in the draft, cables and contracts, but there was no answer. Finally, the Mets asked pitcher Sherman (Roadblock) Jones to call Chacon in Venezuela. Jones reported that Chacon said, "OK," but nothing more.

No one knew what that meant.

Chacon eventually wired that he wanted more money, so the Mets upped their offer. Again, no word from Chacon until spring training had started, and then, according to writer Leonard Shecter's account, Chacon sent this: "I am waiting passage. Elio."

No one knew what that meant, either, but the Mets sent a plane ticket to Chacon's address in Venezuela. Chacon replied with this: "I will reached Monday. Sick parent. Elio."

The Mets learned from the airline that Chacon had booked a flight scheduled to arrive in Tampa late on a Monday night. The traveling secretary went to meet him. Chacon arrived six hours late. He tried to explain, but no one understood.

Elio Chacon
DONALD UHRBROCK/TIME LIFE PICTURES/GETTY IMAGES

Have Car, Will Travel

The Mets had a bus to take the ballplayers from the Colonial to the field and back again. It didn't take them anywhere else. Meals were served in the hotel, and there were businesses within walking distance.

The black neighborhoods, barbershops, restaurants and nightclubs, however, were all on the other side of town. For the black players on the team, life at the Colonial was isolating.

So Charlie Neal, Al Jackson and Sherman Jones pooled their money and bought a car for around $200. Eventually they started driving to the ballpark, giving rides to whoever would fit.

At the end of spring training, they gave the car to one of the hotel's kitchen workers. The next season, they came back to find he had fixed up the jalopy. They wanted it back. He refused.

The Thinking Man's Workout

Jay Hook had it worked out pretty nicely. He was going to graduate school in engineering at Northwestern University, a semester per year in the winter. To stay in shape, he played handball with Ara Parseghian, Bo Schembechler and the rest of the football coaches, and they had taught him some isometric strength-training exercises. Hook did them through the winter and continued his routine when he got to spring training. One day during pitchers-and-catchers, he caught Stengel's eye.

"Hook, what are you doing?" Stengel asked.

Hook explained, and Stengel thought for a minute.

"I'd like you to be our physical conditioning instructor when the regular guys come in here," Stengel said, and Hook agreed.

When the rest of the players arrived in Florida, Hook led them out to the outfield and put them through the exercises he'd been doing all winter.

"I think we did it for two or three days," Hook recalled. "Everybody was so stiff and so sore. Casey came up to me about three days later, and said, 'You can forget doing that physical conditioning stuff, everybody's on their own.'"

Keep It Simple

Casey Stengel, for all his strategies and trickeries, was also prone to simplification. He knew the point of baseball, as utility infielder Rod Kanehl said, was to take a round bat and a round ball and "hit it square." And sometimes Stengel did get as basic as possible.

"Casey would take you out the first day of spring training," Kanehl said. "He would say, 'The object is to start at home and get back to home as quick as possible, and touch all the bases in between. Pretty simple.'"

Like a Steel Trap

Casey Stengel had been around baseball forever, and he remembered most of it. His memory, the computer-like ability to recall which players did what in which situations, had served him well. It drove Brooklyn Dodger Jackie Robinson, who always played against Stengel and never for him, crazy.

In the seventh game of the 1952 World Series, Stengel started a lefty, sent in two right-handers, and then, in the middle of the seventh inning, with the Yankees leading 4-2, sent in left-handed reliever Bob Kuzava to face Duke Snider and Jackie Robinson. Robinson popped up and Billy Martin ran from second base and made the catch on his knees.

"Robinson, until he died, said that Casey [switched pitchers] purposefully to show him up," said Rod Kanehl.

"But Casey, he knew what Kuzava's record was against Robinson. Nowadays they've got a computer. You've got books and maps, and you've got it all. Well, back in 62, we didn't have that equipment. Your manager had to know what your record was against certain players. Your managers had to remember."

And Stengel did.

Dollars and Sense

When it came to baseball, Casey Stengel was an encyclopedia. He knew all the players and their tendencies. Stengel had it all in his head, and he had worked out a dollar value for it, too.

In spring training, he might walk up to pitcher Ray Daviault and say, "You don't have a change-up. Now, if you had a change-up, you might have won three more games last year, and instead of being 3-10, you'd be 6-7, and you could ask for $25,000 instead of $18,000."

He might walk up to infielder Rod Kanehl and ask the rhetorical question, "How many bunt singles did you have last year?" Stengel knew exactly how many. He would follow up with this: "If you got five more hits a year, instead of hitting .263, you would hit .275, and instead of making $11,000, you could be making $15,000."

As journalist George Vecsey wrote, one of the first things Stengel told his players in spring training was, "Bust your ass for me and I'll get you more money."

The Casey Stengel All-Night Express

Stengel, in addition to being a talker, was a night person. He would talk as long as someone was around to listen, and for the reporters, who genuinely enjoyed him and were also looking for information, staying up with Stengel became a ritual. The coaches hung around, too.

"He's tough to stay up with at night," Solly Hemus said. "He didn't drink hard, he just liked to talk. And he only needed a couple hours of sleep, he's the darnedest person I ever met in my life. He got two hours sleep, that was plenty. He was a marvel at that, he was always fresh and alert."

Stengel did nap on the bench from time to time. It was one of those things that no one believed until they saw it for themselves.

"One day, Charlie Neal came over to me and he said, 'Our manager is asleep,'" said infielder Felix Mantilla. "I said, 'You've got to be kidding me.' And he pointed, and there he was. It was only the fifth inning. Solly Hemus, he'd take over."

There was no napping for Stengel's coaches. They were out running drills and correcting swings and adjusting motions with no more sleep than Stengel had gotten. Only later would they admit to the players how flat-out exhausted they were.

Stengel's cat naps became a running joke with the players.

Don Zimmer, who was having an excellent spring training, used to sneak up behind Stengel when he was sleeping. Zimmer would shout and clap his hands, and Stengel would jump up, startled, and knock his head on the dugout.

"He fell for that so many times, you wouldn't believe it," pitcher Clem Labine said.

If You Were My Age, You'd Sleep Too

Stengel's mid-afternoon naps didn't stop after spring training. He even fell asleep during games from time to time.

"Then he'd hear the crack of the bat, and he'd sit up and say, 'That's the way, fellers,'" Joe Ginsberg said. "And we'd say, 'Well, Casey, that was the other team.'"

The jokes had leaked into the public realm and the press had some fun at Stengel's expense too. The 72-year-old manager didn't like it, and called a meeting before a game in Los Angeles. He called very few meetings, so the players knew it was important.

"You know, you guys claim that I sleep on the bench," Stengel told them. "I haven't come out in the press and said, when you're as old as I am, and you have to stay up as late as I do to check you guys in at night on the road, you'd sleep too."

Teach the Children

Clem Labine and Joe Ginsberg were two of the older players to be invited to Mets spring training. They didn't get to play much. As veterans, Stengel asked them to help out with the youngest players, most of whom would not make the team either. It was a raw deal for Labine and Ginsberg, though they made the best of it.

"Stengel said, 'Joe, I want you to help with the catchers, and Clem, you're the oldest pitcher here, and I want you to help with these youngsters,'" Labine said. "Here we are becoming coaches instead of players. So we did. When spring training games started, all of a sudden we're relegated not to play in the games but to stay with the kids. So they would go off and play and we would take the kids from about eight o'clock in the morning til about one in the afternoon. Then Joe and I would go play golf, instead of doing what we should have been doing, which was practicing our trade."

Clem Labine
DONALD UHRBROCK/TIME LIFE PICTURES/GETTY IMAGES

But for Their Own Integrity

Casey Stengel didn't have many rules for his players, but he had a couple: no spikes in the clubhouse and no drinking in the hotel.

Joe Ginsberg and Clem Labine came in for dinner late one night after a long round of golf. The only people left in the dining room were Stengel, his wife Edna and some of the reporters. The pitcher and catcher sat at a separate table.

"All of a sudden, the waitress came over to us and said, 'Mr. Stengel would like to buy you a drink.'" Labine recalled. "We looked at each other and Joe said, 'Well, let's have a beer.' And that was it. We waved to Casey, and he waved back to us."

The next day Stengel called a meeting before practice. "Something happened last night," he told the team. "And you know what my rules are in this place. We had two ballplayers go in that dining room last night and they were drinking beer, and it's going to cost them $50 each. Okay, you two guys stand up."

No one stood up.

"You know who you are," Stengel said. Labine and Ginsberg fessed up, but to this day Labine maintains that Stengel could not remember which ballplayers he'd tricked into breaking the rules.

Lesson Learned

The veterans took care of the rookies off the field as well. At least at first, an older player roomed with a younger player, to show him the ropes.

Rookie lefty Al Jackson shared a room at spring training with veteran first-baseman Charlie Neal, who was partial to room service. Neal ordered food to the room regularly, which seemed a nice perk to Jackson.

One night Jackson decided he too would order from the room service menu. Neal told him he was crazy. Neal knew what rookie pitchers earned, and it wasn't enough to mortgage the good life.

"Go downstairs," Neal said.

Chastened, Jackson headed to the team's dining room off the hotel restaurant. When he tried to order food to the room some time later, Neal again sent him right down to the restaurant. "He said I couldn't afford room service, and he was right," acknowledged Jackson.

Charlie Neal
DONALD UHRBROCK/TIME LIFE PICTURES/GETTY IMAGES

Johnny Pappas, Honorary Met

For someone who never even played a professional baseball game, let alone put on a Met uniform, Johnny Pappas is as much a part of that first spring training as any of the players who did. The tall skinny kid from New York paid his own way to St. Petersburg in late February. He wanted to be a Met. He had no organized baseball experience. He'd been throwing under the bridges in snowy New York.

At first, Johnny Murphy, an assistant to Weiss, told him to get lost.

But some of the writers got wind of Pappas's story, and convinced Murphy to give him a tryout. It wasn't like the Mets didn't need the help.

Pappas wasn't any good. Murphy sent him home, but the writers had their story. It was as good a public relations move as any the team could have orchestrated. Who couldn't love a team like this?

The Mass Media

There were a handful of players in spring training who had played for the Dodgers. They were used to the New York press corps. The rest of the team came from cities and towns where at most one or two reporters covered baseball for the local papers. They were stunned and amazed by the sheer number of reporters—probably two dozen—who were there to cover the team.

"On the field, the baseball was the same," said Jim Hickman. "There was a lot more media hype than I was used to. You know, in the minor leagues, you don't get much of that. Then you go to the city with probably the most media in the entire country, and it's a bit of a change."

The reporters were happy to be there, and the press box at Miller Huggins field contained a pretty high concentration of talent. Among others: from the *Daily News,* Dick Young, who was considered by many to be the most influential baseball writer in the country; for the *Long Island Press,* Jack Lang, who had been covering New York baseball since 1946; for *Newsday,* columnist Stan Isaacs; Robert Lipsyte for the *New York Times*; Leonard Shecter for the *New York Post.*

Old Home Week

A lot of the reporters assigned to the Mets had covered the Dodgers or the Giants. When those teams moved west, their newspapers were suddenly saddled with National League baseball writers without a National League team to write about. These were writers used to competing for stories on the front page—or in at the New York tabloids, the back page. In the intervening years, most had covered the Yankees, along with whoever was already covering the team. They were glad to have a show of their own again.

"I didn't particularly care for the American League, but I had some good friends over there," he said. "Whitey Ford was a good friend of mine before he started playing ball, and knowing Whitey, you got to know Mickey and Roger. But it was good to get back to the National League, because I had covered them for so long with the Dodgers. I liked National League ball better too. I also knew people in the National League, employees and scouts and managers. I grew up a National League fan. It was more to my liking."

The Cameras Don't Lie

The television stations were there, too, and sometimes the cameras could not make the Mets into fantastical poetry the way the writers could. One day Channel 9—the Mets' broadcast channel in New York—was filming practice. The catchers were working on fundamentals, shagging pop-ups at that particular moment. The wind was gusting 15 to 20 miles an hour, wreaking havoc on the drill.

Lindsey Nelson was interviewing catcher Hobie Landrith. Behind him, catcher Joe Ginsberg was running around in circles trying to catch fly balls. Eventually, he circled behind Nelson, tripped and fell.

Landrith said gamely, "Well, we've got some things to work on."

No one watching could keep a straight face. That should have been an omen right there.

An Inauspicious Start

The Mets played their first spring training game on March 10 and lost to St. Louis 8-0. There was a 56-piece brass band and baseball commissioner Ford Frick addressed the crowd.

Charlie Neal got the first hit, an infield single in the first inning. Roger Craig was supposed to pitch the first game, but he had injured his neck the day before, so Jay Hook threw the first pitch in Mets history.

By the time the Cardinals took a 7-0 lead in the fifth inning, people started to head for the exits. "Same old Mets," muttered one on his way out.

Winning Streak

With their first loss behind them, the Mets went on to win three straight spring training games. On March 11, they beat St. Louis 4-3 in the ninth inning, when Richie Ashburn scored on a single by Elio Chacon. Choo Choo Coleman hit the club's first home run in the eighth, erasing a 3-0 St. Louis lead. They won two more before the Dodgers—their B team—got the better of the Mets.

Dinner with the Boss

Mrs. Payson watched a lot of games that spring training, scorecard in hand, pencil in teeth. The players were impressed that a lady with so much money could be so down to earth. One night after a win, she was so pleased that she took the whole team out to dinner. They found a steakhouse that looked like it would suit everybody.

"We weren't sure if the restaurants around there would serve the black players," Felix Mantilla said. "Mrs. Payson went in and she said, 'Are you going to allow the whole team in here?' And they did."

Mrs. Payson sat right down with the players and ordered up a steak.

"I was sitting next to her, or one over from her," said Frank Thomas. "The waitress asked her what she wanted, and she said steak. [The waitress] asked her how she wanted it, and she said, 'Just cut off its horns, wipe its fanny, and bring it out.'"

Playing Cards, Passing Time

The spring season forged all kinds of friendships. Judy Anderson joined her husband Craig in the team dining room every night for dinner, and the team got to know the pitcher and his wife as a couple. They were just learning to play bridge and found no shortage of foursomes on the Mets. Gil Hodges told Anderson that the Dodgers had been pretty big bridge players, and one night Hodges and coach Cookie Lavagetto sat down to play bridge.

It was a social time, Anderson said. "We got to know Stengel and [his wife] Edna, and then all the players, except maybe those who lived off with their wives. It was different. You got to know the players maybe a little better than you would have, and you found out all these stories about these guys."

Grandma and Grandpa Stengel

Even players who set up their own domiciles with wives and children found their lives touched by the easy-going atmosphere of spring training. Jay Hook and his wife Joan often ate dinner in local restaurants, toddlers Marcy and Wes in tow.

"Joan would always have the kids looking really nice for supper," Hook recalled. "Marcy would be in a dress, and Wes would have a pair of shorts on or something."

One night the Hook family, looking sharp, ran into Stengel and Edna while they were out for supper. Stengel came over to say hello, then suggested they bring the children to meet Edna. The Stengels never had any children, and they were always open to surrogates.

"From then on, whenever Casey and Edna would see our kids, they'd come over and talk to them," Hook said. "The kids would go off with them, walking around or whatever. The kids looked at Casey and Edna as another set of grandparents. It really was a nice relationship."

A Hard Lesson

Jay Hook was having a good time in spring training. He and his wife and their two kids had found a little house on the beach in St. Petersburg, a manageable bike ride from the field. Days were for baseball, and Hook even managed to get a hitting lesson or two from Rogers Hornsby, arguably one of baseball's best second baseman, and the Mets new hitting coach.

"I thought, if I can improve my bunting and hitting, maybe I can stay in games longer, because maybe they won't take me out for a pinch-hitter as quick. And I think it worked that way," Hook said. "Hornsby was a terrific hitter. And I thought, you know, it'd be good to seek as much knowledge as I could from him."

In late March, all the batting practice in the world couldn't save the pitcher. Stengel left Hook in for six innings against the Orioles, in which he gave up 16 runs on 17 hits. Stengel made Hook suffer through the full sixth inning, when Hook gave up nine hits and eight runs. The Mets lost 18-8.

"It was a terrible game," Hook said. "I didn't have a thing, and Casey left me in there. They were pounding the ball."

At the time Stengel explained that he wanted the relatively young pitcher to get the work in. "Anyway," Stengel told reporters, "I kept thinking he'd get the last five batters out."

The Big Game

No one ought to care about the result of spring training games. Case in point: the Reds, which won the 1961 pennant, lost four of their first five spring training games in 1962, succeeding only in beating the Mets in that stretch. No one was worried about them.

"Spring training is really just to get in shape," Solly Hemus said. "I don't think you can put much rights to it, as far as the future of the ball club and spring training. You can compare the players, but I don't think there are many big games in spring training."

One game did matter. Mets versus Yankees was as big as spring training games get. It was certainly a good sign when the Mets shrugged off a short losing streak with a 1-0 win over the Tigers the day before the Yankees came to town.

A Moral Victory

The game didn't matter, Stengel told reporters. But he saved his two best pitchers, Roger Craig and Al Jackson, to pitch in the Mets' first spring training game with the Yankees and managed his way to a 4-3 win with a dramatic ninth inning.

In the top of the ninth, Yankees second baseman Bobby Richardson hit a two-out single to score third baseman Clete Boyer and tie the score. Stengel sent Howie Nunn, who didn't ultimately make the 1962 Mets roster, to relieve Al Jackson, who had pitched nearly three good innings of relief. Nunn got a pop-up for the third out. He only faced one batter. He still got the win.

Joe Christopher opened the bottom of the inning with a triple. Don Zimmer flied out. Stengel sent Richie Ashburn to pinch-hit for Nunn. Ashburn had sat out the beginning of the game with a sore hip, but he didn't have to do much. He nailed Gary Blaylock's first pitch into center field and Christopher crossed the plate with the winning run.

Stengel was in his element after his new club beat his old club. He stayed on the field forever doing interviews with writers and television and radio broadcasters. That night, the Mets held a cocktail party.

"Julie Adler had been with the *Times*, but he was the promotion director with the Mets. He called New York," recalled Jack Lang. "He called [the famous sports bar] Toots Shor's. Toots said it was like New Year's Eve at the bar. They were five deep at the bar. All the National League fans came out of the woodwork. The Mets beat the famous Yankees."

Already, the shouts could be heard all the way up the eastern seaboard: "Break up the Mets."

Momentum

Beating the Yankees did the Mets a world of good. They beat the Dodgers by the same score (4-3) the next day, even without fielding many of their better players, though Gus Bell and Frank Thomas both hit run-scoring singles in the third. The next day they showed they could not only beat the good teams but the bad ones, too. They knocked Kansas City, which had finished last in the American League in 1961, for a 14-7 win.

And That's Enough of That

The Mets' best winning streak of the spring ended at four wins. They took a lead in the ninth, then gave it right back to the Senators, who won 9-8. Hobie Landrith also distinguished himself as the first Met to get tossed from a game, when umpire Bill Haller fingered Landrith for caustic remarks from the dugout. Landrith insisted it wasn't him and even offered up some of his teammates; Haller sent Landrith, who wasn't in the lineup, to the clubhouse.

Rod Kanehl, Right at Home

Most of the ballplayers who played for Stengel had a hard time understanding exactly what he meant when he said it. Rod Kanehl never had a problem. The infielder had come up through the Yankees system and met Stengel at a rookie camp in 1954. Both were from the Midwest, Stengel from Kansas City, Kanehl from Wichita. And Kanehl's father had been, like Stengel, a coach. The two hit it off immediately.

"One of the conditions of my signing (with the Yankees in '54) was that I would go to the advanced rookie camp in St. Petersburg," Kanehl said. "Which was a real break for me. It was hands-on with Stengel. He ran those advance camps. I would listen to everything he'd say. I was brand new, I mean brand new to professional baseball. I'd played American Legion baseball but track was my main sport."

Kanehl impressed Stengel, and even though he never made the Yankees' major league roster, Stengel remembered him when expansion came around.

The rest of the Mets were amazed by Kanehl's ability to understand and connect with Stengel.

"Hot Rod [Kanehl] had a way of doing things that Stengel liked," said Craig Anderson. "He bunted good, he ran pretty good, he kind of did the little things. Stengel was a perfectionist on the fundamentals. And I learned that from him. He didn't always communicate properly, but he knew baseball. Anybody who did the things like that, Casey really liked. I think that's why [Kanehl] made the club. The rest of us had no clue what Casey liked, we just did the best we could and tried to figure out what he wanted."

Rod Kanehl
Brace Photo

One Lucky Hit

Near the end of spring training, it seemed 26-year-old Rod Kanehl was destined for another season in the minors. The Yankees had just evened up the spring training series with a 3-2 win in Fort Lauderdale, and Kanehl forgot his troubles with a night on the town. He wasn't in the lineup for the next day's game against the Dodgers.

March 28 dawned hot and sunny. Sandy Koufax pitched for Los Angeles, which took a 3-1 lead into the ninth inning. Koufax wanted to finish the game, but he was getting tired. He walked Gil Hodges and Jim Hickman to open the inning, and John DeMerit moved them into scoring position with a sacrifice bunt. Catcher Chris Cannizaro flied out and it looked like Koufax was going to get out of the inning with the victory.

With two out, Stengel called on Kanehl to pinch-hit. He had been close to dozing off in the corner of the dugout. Getting up to hit against Koufax was dizzying.

But he lined a curve-ball down the first-base line, scoring Hodges and Hickman, and Kanehl pulled into second base standing up. Mantilla singled him home for the winning run.

The game had been televised in New York. Kanehl didn't have a big-league contract yet, and he didn't get one until the team was back in New York, but as far as anyone was concerned, he was a Met.

"I was a shoo-in from that point on," Kanehl said. "New Yorkers wondered who this Kanehl was. We beat the Dodgers and that was a big thing."

Optimism Blooms in Springtime

Spring training ended without much fanfare, but the Mets were generating the tiniest bit of optimism. The Mets went on to beat the Phillies in extra innings, and Sherman Jones pitched a nine-inning shutout against the Cardinals; they dropped a game to the Reds, and a ninth-inning four-run rally fell short against Kansas City.

They finished their exhibition season with 12 wins and 15 losses, not bad for an expansion club. Kanehl had hit .440, Zimmer .400. No one could say, however, how well they'd do in the regular season.

Maybe they could at least finish ahead of Houston's expansion team, which was a bunch of no-name players, and the mismanaged Cubs. The Phillies didn't have a good team either. Could they finish as high as seventh?

Chapter
6

BACK TO NEW YORK

Homeward Bound

The Mets flew home from spring training via Portsmouth, Virginia, where rain cancelled a scheduled exhibition game with the Baltimore Orioles. The team flew from there to New York and landed at Idlewild Airport (now John F. Kennedy). After the Mets made their way through the construction, they emerged into the terminal.

Only a handful of people were waiting for the Mets that Sunday evening. Homecoming celebrations befitting the newest team in the biggest American city were planned for Thursday, after the Mets returned from their season-opener in St. Louis. The party would have to wait.

The Mets Take Manhattan

The team stayed that first night at the Waldorf Astoria in Midtown Manhattan. Some of the Mets were in New York for the first time.

"I'm a farm boy from Kentucky," said pitcher Herb Moford. "Any time I was there I was afraid to get too far away from my teammates. I was afraid I'd get lost. Bob Moorhead and me, we were kind of rookies, you'd call us." Moford added that he and Moorhead were occasionally called the "M & M boys," a mildly sarcastic riff on their alphabetical counterparts, the pair of home-run hitters in the Bronx.

That first night, Rod Kanehl took himself on a long walk and didn't blink once.

"I walked out of there and I walked for hours," he remembered. "I walked up 59th Street and I took a left on Seventh Avenue and there's Carnegie Hall. I'm walking around seeing things I'd heard and read about all my life. New York is just amazing to someone from the Midwest."

Home at Home

On their first day in New York, the Mets took a look around the Polo Grounds. Clem Labine and the other former Dodgers found out the home team's clubhouse was just as dilapidated as the visitors' was. Gil Hodges picked up a bat, stepped into the batter's box and swung for the fences. The field held generally good memories for the team's veterans.

"I wish our young players, right now, I wish they could get lucky enough to see such a park as the Polo Grounds," reminisced Don Zimmer. "It was a very unique ballpark. Their eyes open when I say 260 down the left field line, 280 down the right field line. But you better hit 'em down the lines because you need a cab ride to hit it over the center field fence. It was a very unique park. I think of it all the time."

Hit This Sign

The Mets were also discovering some of the incentives and contests awaiting them in the stadium. Howard Clothes, the Mets' sponsor that had given them office space, hung a sign down the lines of the Polo Grounds. A ball that hit the sign was worth one point; one that hit the eight-foot yellow circle earned the batter five points. At the end of the season, the Met with the most points won a $7,000 motor boat.

There were more inducements in the outfield. Bohack's supermarket offered 10,000 King Korn trading stamps for a home run, 50,000 for a grand slam.

One of the Mets sponsors seemed to be making it harder to hit, rather than easier. Rheingold, the official beer of the Mets, hung a gleaming white sign straight out in center field, with Rheingold across it in red script. The glare of the sun off the sign blinded batters almost 500 feet away. The Mets didn't need that kind of headache. Eventually the sign was removed.

Get Me Outta Here!

The Mets flew to St. Louis to get the business of major league baseball underway. It would be harder than they expected. First, there was the matter of getting to their rooms. A dozen or so Mets crammed into the elevator at their hotel and promptly got stuck there.

"We had just gotten there, and everybody jammed on the elevator," Jay Hook remembered. "It wasn't like it was just a few guys. We were packed in there like sardines. When the elevator got stuck, you can imagine all the comments, with a bunch of guys on the elevator. They punched the emergency button, but we didn't know that the microphone in the elevator that you could talk into went right into the lobby of the hotel. So all these comments, that the guys were making, were being heard in the lobby. They were swearing, and as you would imagine, (there were) a few crude comments. I can't remember if there was anybody else on the elevator besides ballplayers, but if there was I feel sorry for them."

The trapped Mets finally got out of the elevator 20 minutes later, only to be rained out of their first game.

The Feller in Right Field

Reporters had been asking Casey Stengel about his opening lineup for at least a week. It drove him nuts, as he was prone to making last-minute changes and probably didn't finalize the card until the game was less than a day away. Finally, he gave the lineup on the air with the Mets broadcasters.

"Lindsey [Nelson] did an interview with Casey Stengel in our first broadcast," recalled Ralph Kiner. "He asked Casey to name the starters. And [Stengel] went on for 23 minutes by the clock. He started with the catcher and he said, uttering his now famous phrase, 'You've gotta have a catcher, if you don't have a catcher you're going to have a lot of passed balls,' and he went on to first base, second, short, and went to everywhere on the field except the right fielder. After 23 minutes, Lindsey said to him, 'Casey, you mentioned everyone except who's going to play right field.' Well, Casey couldn't think of his name. So he started out, 'The fellow out there, he played with the Pittsburgh Pirates and the Cincinnati Reds,' and he went on and on, etcetera, etcetera. Finally he said, '… and when he hits it he'll ring a bell and that's his name, Gus Bell.'"

Gus Bell
DONALD UHRBROCK/TIME LIFE PICTURES/GETTY IMAGES

Roadblock's False Start

Sherman (Roadblock) Jones was slated to start the first game against the Cardinals, leaving ex-Dodger and staff ace Roger Craig well-rested for the home opener. But Jones was accident-prone. He'd taken a line drive in the shins in spring training, which put him on crutches and sidelined him for 10 days. He was healthy and ready to play by the time the team went to Portsmouth, Virginia, for an exhibition game; while there, Jones temporarily blinded himself when he was lighting a cigarette and the match-head flew off and struck him in the eye. The trainers gave him a gauze eye patch. Roger Craig got the start in St. Louis.

For those keeping score at home, the Mets' lineup in their first-ever game was:

Richie Ashburn, centerfield

Felix Mantilla, shortstop

Charlie Neal, second base

Frank Thomas, left field

Gus Bell, right field

Gil Hodges, first base

Don Zimmer, third base

Hobie Landrith, catcher

Roger Craig, pitcher

Just because they started the game, didn't mean they finished. Stengel was already up to his signature managerial tricks. Ed Bouchee and Jim Marshall both pinch-hit; Bob Moorhead, Clem Labine and Herb Moford pitched in relief.

St. Louis mayor Raymond R. Tucker threw out the first pitch. It was 55 degrees and muddy, with more than 16,000 in attendance.

Broadcaster Bob Murphy kicked off the Mets inaugural season with these inauspicious words: "This is Bob Murphy, welcoming you to the first regular-season game in the history of the New York Mets. Tonight the New York Mets meet the St. Louis Cardinals right here in St. Louis."

0-and-One

The Cardinals were considered pennant contenders. Roger Craig started the game with a sour note, giving up two runs in the first inning, the second one on a balk. He lasted just three innings. By the time he was finished, he'd given up eight hits and five runs, and St. Louis was well on its way to an 11-4 victory. The Mets, for their part, allowed three stolen bases and made three errors, including a costly misplay at second base by Charlie Neal, who let a grounder slide right by him to begin the Cardinals' four-run sixth inning.

George Weiss sat bundled up in the St. Louis stands, but the rest of the top brass was spared. Mrs. Payson and the rest of the top owners had flown to Missouri for the first game but returned to New York when it was rained out.

A Welcome Fit for a Champion

The Mets returned to New York 0-1, but the new team came home to the kind of celebration the city usually reserved for its world champions.

New York hosted a ticker-tape parade for the Mets straight up lower Broadway. Casey Stengel was drum major and emcee all in one, riding on the first float, waving, and tossing plastic baseballs to the crowd. The players followed, riding in convertibles that alternated with brass bands. In spite of the snowy forecast, an estimated 40,000 people turned out to cheer for the Mets and the return of National League baseball.

"They couldn't have picked a better manager to lead the parade down Broadway," said Rod Kanehl. "The fans loved him. You know, they didn't necessarily love him when he was a Yankee manager, but he was different when he was with the Mets. He was more patient. He knew that he didn't have the ball club, that we didn't have any pitching."

Word had it the Yankees weren't too happy about the Mets' extravagant welcome home. The last time the Bombers received that kind of public enthusiasm was mid-summer 1949; from October 1949 to April 1962 they had won eight World Series—but they didn't get a single ticker-tape parade. The Mets hadn't even won a game!

Off and Running

Maybe it was an omen for the season ahead. At the time, it just seemed like disorganization, miscommunication, or plain dumb luck.

When the Mets showed up at the Polo Grounds after their ticker-tape parade, they waited an hour for their spikes to arrive. They'd worn street shoes for the ceremonies and left their spikes at the Hotel Manhattan. Stengel also locked himself out of his office.

The Pittsburgh Pirates, who had won the pennant the year before, weren't having a much better time of it. They had arrived at the Polo Grounds for practice, only to find that the visitor's locker room was still under construction, and went back to their hotel.

The Pirates Return

There was an interesting symmetry in the Pirates' return to New York to open the Mets' season. The Pirates had closed out the Giants' residency in New York, with a 9-1 win on Sept. 29, 1957. Johnny Antonelli, whom the Mets had tried to sign, was the Giants' losing pitcher that day. Frank Thomas, who made the final put-out for the Pirates in that game, was now playing for the Mets.

"I was playing first base," said Thomas, who pocketed the baseball after the game. "Tommy Henrich asked me for the baseball, and I gave it to him. I understand it sold for $15,000 not too long ago."

Superstitious? Who's Superstitious?

By the way, the Mets opened at home on April 13—a Friday. Arthur Daley of the *Times* wrote: "Only the most contemptible of cads would attempt to read any significance into (that) fact ... The National League is back in our town. That is the only thing that is important."

We Interrupt
Our Regularly Scheduled Programming...

That day, nothing went smoothly. Even the broadcasters, who were some of the best in the business, had some kinks to work out.

"My first interview on TV was with Casey Stengel at that first game at home," Ralph Kiner said. "And the big word with Casey Stengel was to get him off the air on time, because everything's segmented in a 15-minute slot. He finally stopped talking; he was aware he should stop, and I thanked him very much. We were using lavaliere microphones, and he got up and walked off the set. When he walked away, he was still attached and he pulled the whole set down. It crashed to the floor. Our assistant director, Ralph Robbins, he was panic-stricken. He didn't know what to do. We had cue cards at that time, and I was supposed to go to a commercial. So I said, 'When my AD holds up the cue cards, I'll tell you what's coming up next.' That was all I could do."

With No Shortage of Ceremony

The Manhattan and Queens borough presidents brought presents for Stengel before the home opener with Pittsburgh; Mrs. Payson received a plaque from a group of ex-Giant fans; M. Donald Grant made a speech.

With the exception of first baseman Jim Marshall, pitcher Sherman Jones, and catcher Joe Ginsberg, the Mets fielded the same lineup for their home opener as they had in St. Louis.

"I'll never forget it," Ginsberg said. "Casey called me and he said, 'You've had 13 years in the big leagues, and I want you to catch the first game in New York. You'll get more credit for that than anything else in those 13 years.'"

Roadblock's Reflections

"It wasn't a big crowd for the Polo Grounds," recalled Sherman Jones, thinking about the Mets' first home game. But I guess people didn't want to get damp and wet. And the Pirates were to be my victims. It didn't turn out that way, but I handled them pretty good, I thought.

"I don't recall being nervous, but probably I was in the beginning, I would think. Looking back at it all these years, I would probably be a little nervous, but it wore off, because I made my living doing that."

Jones pitched for the Mets, and Tom Sturdivant started for the Pirates. The Mets lost 4-3 on a slick and muddy field. With two outs in the second inning, Pirates catcher Smoky Burgess hit a line drive to Charlie Neal, who made the stop, then couldn't quite pivot in the mud. He pulled Jim Marshall off the bag with the throw; Burgess scored on a Don Hoak double. Bill Mazeroski was up next, and he hit a fly ball to right center. Gus Bell waved away Richie Ashburn, then let the pop-up drop; Hoak scored and Mazeroski went to third.

Jones was out after five innings (five hits, two runs, one walk) and Frank Thomas hit his first home run of the season in the sixth.

"Who hit the first home run in the Polo Grounds" Jones asked. "Well, Frank Thomas. But who got the first base hit in the Polo Grounds? I did. I was a pretty good hitter. Later on in the years, I found out I'd had the first hit. I still have a clipping of that article."

The Mets never pulled ahead. Relievers Herb Moford and Ray Daviault both struggled with their deliveries in the mud; in the span of four batters, Daviault walked one and threw two wild pitches.

The Mets pulled within one in the bottom of the ninth inning. With two out, Don Zimmer, representing the tying run, went to first on an infield single. Joe Ginsberg popped out to end it.

Sherman Jones
BRACE PHOTO

It Wouldn't Be New York if the Fans Didn't Boo

It was not all cheers, though. New Yorkers like to boo. The 12,447 who braved the elements jeered Mayor Robert Wagner, a lefty, who threw out the first pitch. They booed Jim Marshall, in the lineup at first base in place of ex-Dodger Gil Hodges, who begged off with a sore knee. Gus Bell, the right fielder, heard jeers from the crowd when he let a catchable fly ball drop, turning it into a run-scoring triple.

The fans were willing to cheer just about anything that could be construed as good for the Mets. Richie Ashburn got a standing ovation when he singled in the first Mets run in the fifth; the crowd cheered for called strikes when the Mets were in the field, turned on a dime when they were up to bat and yelled encouragement for called balls. Daviault heard his share of jeering for his wild pitches, but the crowd reversed itself enthusiastically when he got the final Pittsburgh batter out.

Richie Ashburn
BRACE PHOTO

Typical Stengel

The following story lives on from the opening series with Pittsburgh.

Herb Moford relieved Sherman Jones after the fifth inning of the opener. Jones was losing 2-1. Moford gave up one run in the sixth and none in the seventh, but by then he was at the top of the batting order. New franchise, first game at home, fresh pitching staff—everything suggested Stengel ought to pinch-hit for Moford. Stengel's coaching staff cornered him in the dugout, all talking at once.

"You've got to pinch hit for Moford."

And, "Who do you want to hit for Moford?"

And, "You've got to get a pinch-hitter."

Stengel let his staff do a lot of coaching, but he didn't like to be told what to do. He was still in charge. Craig Anderson tells the end of the story like this:

"(Stengel) comes down our way, and he goes over to Moford who was standing there. 'Hey Herb,' he said, 'Are you a good hitter?'

"If you're an old pitcher and you're asked if you're a good hitter, you always say yes. You're never going to say 'No, I'm a lousy hitter,' because you want to stay in the game. So Herb said, 'Yeah, I'm a good hitter.'

"So Stengel says, 'You go ahead and hit.'

"We're all on the bench taking all this in, and I'm getting a kick out of it, a disagreement between coaches. While we're laughing and talking about it, Herb goes up, swings at the first pitch, and gets a base hit. We're all in the dugout, laughing, and we look up, and Stengel put a pinch-runner in. I mean, that's the type of stuff that he did. He let the pitcher hit and he takes him out."

The Future Watched from the Owner's Box

Ed Kranepool, the schoolboy wonder from the Bronx, watched the game with Mrs. Payson in the owner's box. He was seven months shy of his 18th birthday, his final season at James Monroe High School was only just beginning, and graduation was at least two months away, but the Mets were already courting him.

Kranepool's mother Ethel accompanied him to the Polo Grounds for the Mets' debut. Years later, the first baseman told reporters that he didn't recall much about that historic game; his awe and excitement, combined with the passage of time left him remembering that it was so cold he could see his breath, and that the Mets lost.

Kranepool went on to set the James Monroe baseball team's record for home runs in a season. He hit nine, two better than famous Monroe alum Hank Greenberg's seven. On June 27, he signed an amateur free-agent contract for $85,000. It was more than enough for Kranepool to buy a house in White Plains, New York, for his mother and a new Ford Thunderbird for himself.

Nothing Like Bedsheets, Ingenuity and Indelible Ink

Early in the season, a group of fans from New Jersey showed up at the Polo Grounds with a window shade and hung it over the lower deck in left center field. On it, they had written, "We love the Mets" and underneath that, "Hot Rod Kanehl."

"I'm sitting on the bench and (Richie) Ashburn came over to me," Kanehl recalled. "He said, 'What'd that cost you?' I hadn't even seen it, and he said, 'Look up there in left field.' It was kind of exciting. And then people started bringing signs to the games."

The Mets fans started a banner craze. The signs took on their own momentum, and the camera would pan for the cleverest signs during baseball's slow moments, which gave the broadcasters something to talk about other than how badly the Mets were faring. At first, George Weiss and M. Donald Grant tried to have banner bearers ejected. They didn't get it: the carriers were crazy about the underdog Mets. If their team could play valiantly against the rest of major league baseball, then the fans would happily resist the iron fist of Weiss and Grant.

Eventually, the Mets' front office caught on. In 1963, the team held its first "banner day" and encouraged fans to bring signs. The sign-wavers happily responded, parading with their banners around the stadium. It became as fantastic an art exhibition as any in Manhattan's trendy galleries. A young man wearing a yarmulke and traditional Hasidic side-curls carried a sign reading, "Let's go Mets" in English and Yiddish. One interactive sign had a head-sized hole cut-out, with lettering and an arrow pointing to the "typical Mets fan." Others celebrated present or former Mets—"Bring back Butterball Botz" referred to a player who was cut from the team in spring training, 1962. "To err is human, to forgive is a Mets fan" captured perfectly the spirit of the fans.

Chapter
7

THE FIRST WEEK, THE FIRST WIN

0-and-Three

T he Mets didn't win their second home game, either.
Pittsburgh won 6-2. A pitcher named Vinegar Bend
Mizell, who was throwing quite well even though he never
lived up to his 'Left-handed Dizzy Dean' potential, gave up
only four hits in seven innings for the Pirates.

The Mets debuted their left-hander, too, but Al Jackson
didn't fare so well against his old team. After giving up two
runs over the first three innings, he walked Mizell with two
outs in the fourth. That opened the floodgates. Mizell
moved to third on a Bill Virdon double, and Dick Groat
scored them both with a hard grounder past third. Roberto
Clemente sent Groat to third with a double, and Dick Stuart
knocked a ball up the first-base line, scoring Clemente and
Groat. After four innings, the Pirates led, 6-1, and the Mets
weren't coming back.

Playing the Percentages

Platooning had been around for a long time before Casey Stengel became a manager, but he brought the practice back into vogue when he platooned the Yankees in the 1950s. By the '60s, it had caught on with other managers, too, and when Danny Murtaugh brought the Pirates to the Mets' first homestand, both wily managers used the same strategy.

Stengel fielded a right-handed lineup against Mizell. Murtaugh did the same thing against Jackson. As one writer remarked, "The laws of percentage baseball cannot work for two sides at the same time," and Pittsburgh won that first southpaw face-off.

Stengel stuck with his strategy throughout the season. Craig Anderson wondered why.

"He kept platooning the team," Anderson said. "That was the way he coached the Yankees. Well, we didn't have depth, we didn't have a lot of talent, to platoon so much. So in the long run, it seemed like he should have tried to stick with the best nine guys he could've gotten all the time. But that wasn't the way he managed. He managed by always putting the lefties in against the righties."

Onward and Downward

In their fourth game at home, the opener of their first doubleheader, the Mets slipped to 0-4. The weather was chilly, but it seemed the Mets were warming up. Felix Mantilla crushed the first pitch of the first game into the right-field seats, giving the Mets their first-ever lead in a major league game.

They were still the Mets, though. Pittsburgh drilled starter Roger Craig for five runs in the third inning. First Bill Virdon and Dick Groat crossed the plate on a sacrifice fly and a run-scoring single, respectively. Then Smoky Burgess hit a three-run homer to right field. Craig was out by the fourth. Ken MacKenzie was in, and promptly gave up two more runs to give Pittsburgh a 7-1 lead.

Despite the snow-filled gray clouds overhead, the teams started game two. One fan couldn't see all the way to the bullpen and asked his neighbor which pitcher was entering the game.

"Santa Claus," came the reply, as just then, the snow started to fall. The unlucky Mets, of course, had a two-run lead when the game was called in the third inning.

Home Alone

The Mets were making a habit of solo homers. Jim Marshall hit the Mets' sixth home run of the season near the end of the third game with Pittsburgh with nobody on. There was no shortage of big bats in the Mets' lineup, it would turn out. Frank Thomas hit 34 home runs that season, Marv Throneberry hit 16, and Jim Hickman hit 13 homers and 18 doubles. Getting them all hitting at the same time was the hard part.

Injuries Hurt

Gil Hodges was still out of the lineup with a sore knee, and in the aborted second game of the Mets' first doubleheader, the team lost another ex-Dodger, second baseman Charlie Neal. In the first inning, Neal walked. It looked like Frank Thomas's double would send Neal home, but he stopped at third. He'd pulled a muscle in his foot.

Ninth Place

At least the 0-4 Mets weren't in last place yet. Chicago had played more games and hadn't won one, either. At 0-5, the Cubs were definitely tenth. It was a bittersweet ninth for the Mets, though, if they cared to think about it—three of the Cubs' losses were to Houston, the other expansion team, which had no business being better than New York.

According to journalist George Vecsey, an early banner at the Polo Grounds read, "We don't want to set the world on fire, we just want to finish ninth."

Looking for a Place to Stay

Amidst this inauspicious start to the baseball season, the Mets were trying to get settled in New York. Generally baseball clubs helped their players find housing, either through partnerships with rental offices or by simply keeping a list of the places former players had rented. What with all the painting and drafting and getting organized, the Mets had overlooked their players' housing needs.

"I guess they felt, it was a big city, and you would be able to find something," John DeMerit said. "Every place I played had a list of places, and they'd say, take this list, call these people, and you'll be able to find a place to stay. In New York it was, 'Here's the newspaper.' For the front office, it probably wasn't that important, but for ballplayers, it was pretty necessary."

Apartment Wanted

To help the players find places to stay, Jay Hook, who had been elected one of the team's player representatives, approached broadcasters Bob Murphy, Lindsey Nelson, and Ralph Kiner. He explained that the team was, for all intents and purposes, homeless.

"I said, 'Could you announce that there are a number of players looking for housing,'" Hook said. "And you know, we'd appreciate it if people who had housing would call in and let us know."

On April 15, while the Mets were losing 7-2 to Pittsburgh, the broadcasters asked anyone with an available sublet to call the Mets. Soon enough the switchboard at the Mets offices lit up with calls from people who had rooms, apartments and houses for rent.

Nobody warned the Mets operators. They answered the phone, told would-be landlords that they had no idea what they were calling about, and refused to take their messages.

Yes, but Can He Sing?

Meanwhile, Craig Anderson's wife, Judy, and another player's wife were working together to try to find a place to stay. Finally, they went to a real estate agency, where they ran into a problem that seemed to plague the Mets in those early days.

"What does your husband do?" the real estate agent asked Judy.

"He's with the Mets," she replied.

"Oh, is he a tenor, or a bass?" asked the agent, who heard Met, not Mets.

Apartment Wanted, Part II

The first attempt at on-air classified advertising for players' housing was, on its face, a failure, but it did prove that there were plenty of New Yorkers out there with apartments and houses available. The trick was to bring them together with the players who needed them, and that took both the willingness of Mets management and a little strategic grandstanding by Jay Hook.

The Mets were fewer than five days away from their first real road trip of the season, and many of the players, who had hoped to be settled, were still living out of suitcases in hotels.

Hook went to Stengel.

"I said, 'Casey, I don't want to be a pain, but if I don't have a place for my family to stay before we leave town, I'm not going on the road,'" Hook remembered. "Well, he hit the ceiling, you know: 'Don't tell me we're going to have trouble with you and your family.'"

Of course, this was the same family whose tiny children had adopted the Stengels as honorary grandparents during spring training. Hook suspected that Stengel and his wife, Edna, had not found a permanent place to stay either.

So Stengel went to George Weiss and got approval for the switchboard to field calls for prospective housing, and by the end of the next day, the Mets had more than 100 places to see.

"It worked out fine," said Hook. "But that was a problem for a number of guys, because there were a number of guys who had never been in New York before, and they didn't know where to look. And initially, the club didn't give us any help in finding places. And I thought, the clubs should help with that."

New Homes in New York

Eventually all the Mets found places to stay. The Hook family found a house in Ardsley, a town in Westchester County that bordered affluent Scarsdale.

The Andersons hadn't wanted to stay in downtown Manhattan, but a nice apartment opened up and they took it.

Al Jackson's pregnant young wife joined him in New York shortly after opening day, and they stayed on 71st Street, near Charlie Neal.

Ken MacKenzie and his wife found a downtown apartment, and when they got there, a downstairs neighbor welcomed them with a sign in which she professed her support as a Mets fan.

Gil Hodges, of course, went home to Brooklyn.

Jim Hickman stayed at the old Manhattan hotel, on 8th avenue and 42nd street, near where the Port Authority bus station is now.

Rod Kanehl stayed with a cousin on the Upper West Side for the first part of the season, then moved to an apartment on Old Bergen Road in Jersey City when his family joined him. It was the best thing he could afford on his $9,000 salary, even though it was a two-hour commute to the Polo Grounds by public transportation.

John DeMerit found an apartment on Grand Concourse, in the Bronx, an apartment just blocks from Yankee Stadium. DeMerit and his wife frequently took their kids across the street to the park, but they never went to the stadium, he said, until they came back to visit New York many, many years later.

Cold Weather, Cold Feet

Given that the team had yet to win a game, Casey Stengel took every opportunity he could to try to break up the downhill momentum. In other words, the weather was bad, but it wasn't that bad. Stengel called the first game of the Mets' series at home with Houston on account of dampness.

"If we were a winner, I'd play five times a day, because you tend to keep on winning," Stengel told reporters. "But I had a chance to call the game, and I did. You tend to keep losing if you're losing."

The rain out, or drizzle out, as was probably more appropriate, offered a glimmer of hope that Charlie Neal's injured foot would heal in time for the series with the Colt .45s. It didn't.

Yes, but Can Bernoulli Throw a Slider?

Everyone knew Jay Hook played baseball in between semesters at Northwestern University, where he was studying gas dynamics. A baseball player in a physics class was as unusual as a physics student in the clubhouse, so Hook and his friends in graduate school had extrapolated what they knew about Sputnik, the world's first artificial satellite launched by the Russians in 1957, and applied it to the principles governing a curve ball.

One day in spring training, *Journal American* reporter Barney Kremenko approached Hook for a minor physics lesson.

"He said, 'Jay, I just need a couple of lines to finish out this column. I know you know, just give me a couple lines about why a curve ball curves,'" Hook recalled. "So I said a couple things."

A few weeks later, during the team's first rained out game in New York, the *New York Times'* Robert Lipsyte decided to revisit the issue in more depth.

"[Lipsyte] came in and said, 'Hey Jay, I've got 13 inches of column to fill, explain to me why a curve ball curves,'" said Hook. "So he got a piece of paper and a pencil, and I drew a ball, the microscopically rough surface, the boundary buildup, and the pressure gradients, or the velocity gradients on opposite sides of the ball, and therefore the pressure gradients or the force vectors on the ball. And I wrote out Bernoulli's law, which is just a physical law that governs why an airplane wing lifts a plane."

Lipsyte didn't take Hook's word for it. He took the pitcher's sketches over to the physics department at Columbia University, and associate professor Gerald Feinberg confirmed the accuracy of Hook's drawings.

The next day, Lipsyte's story ran in the *Times* with the headline, "Hook hopes to use Bernoulli's Law in Mets' Game Today." Later Lipsyte told Hook he'd won $100 from the paper for best article of the month.

Houston, We Have a Problem

Even a perfect explanation of the physical laws governing a curve ball couldn't save Jay Hook on the mound. On April 17 he pitched all right in the first game with Houston —went eight innings, gave up six hits and two runs—but the Mets lost anyway, 5-2, in the 11th inning. It was the first time they had gone to extra innings, and the Mets were beginning to make confusion a trademark of their ballgames. The Mets scored their first run in the bottom of the eighth inning, when Mantilla, running from third, met Houston catcher Hal Smith on the base path. Mantilla hit the ground, and Smith thought he'd made the tag and tossed the ball to third base. Realizing that Smith had not tagged him at all, Mantilla got up and ran home.

Herb Moford pitched the last three innings and took the loss. Gus Bell tied it with a home run to right field in the ninth; Don Buddin hit a three-run home run in the 11th inning to break the deadlock.

"Houston was terrible," Rod Kanehl said. "We never could beat Houston."

No Rest for the Weary

Houston came and went after a single game, leaving the Mets to contend with St. Louis. The Cardinals were no expansion team. They had ruined the New Yorkers' major league debut with an 11-4 rout. Now they came to New York for more of the same, outscoring the Mets 24-9 in two games (15-5; 9-4).

While in town, St. Louis improved its winning streak to five games. Stan Musial continued his march toward the record books. The future Hall of Famer hit a single in the fifth inning of the second game, tying Babe Ruth for second place in all-time total bases with 5,793. Ty Cobb was still in first place, with 5,863.

On their own march into record books, the Mets were starting to do some things right. It was just a matter of doing all—or most, at least—of the right things at the same time. They continued to hit home runs, for one thing: Ed Bouchee hit two, and Frank Thomas hit three against St. Louis, placing him atop baseball's leaders in that category and giving the Mets 11 in their first seven games. Bouchee's home run in the first game was the Mets' first with men on base. And five was the most runs they'd scored in a game so far. A victory seemed right around the corner.

0-162?

During the Mets' losing streak to open the season, many wondered if the Mets could lose all their games. Casey Stengel, at least, considered the possibility.

"This sets up the possibility of losing 162 games," he said. "Which would probably be a record in the National League, at least."

Respite, Halfway Around the World

Mrs. Payson had by now abandoned her fledgling baseball team in New York, preferring instead to vacation aboard her yacht in the Greek Islands.

She asked to be sent a wire after every game. Accounts differ as to how much detail Mrs. Payson really wanted— some suggest she only wanted the scores, others claimed she taught her chauffer her specific method of keeping a scorecard, so that he could follow the game, then wire her the results of every at-bat.

Apparently even the bright waters of the Mediterranean couldn't ease the angst of the Mets' biggest fan. Eventually, word came from overseas: please don't wire again, until the Mets win a game.

Going for the Record, in Pittsburgh

They couldn't go on losing forever. But if the Mets were going to win, no one expected them to do it in Pittsburgh. The Pirates had opened the season with eight straight wins, including a two-game sweep of the Mets in the Polo

Grounds. They were headed for the Brooklyn Dodgers' 1955 National League record of 10 straight wins to start the season. The Mets, on the other hand, were heading for their own National League watermark: the 1918 Brooklyn Dodgers (who were then called the Robins) and the 1919 Boston Braves shared the record for most consecutive losses at the beginning of a season, with nine. As it was, their chances in Pittsburgh didn't look good, and their next opponent, Cincinnati, had won the pennant the year before. The earliest the Mets could be expected to win a game was a week later, at home, against Philadelphia.

Hitting Their Marks

Pittsburgh and the Mets both tied their records after the first two games. Pittsburgh won the first 8-4 and the second 4-3, for 10 straight wins, handing the Mets their eighth and ninth straight losses. They found themselves in the peculiar position of being 9-1/2 games out of first place, even though they'd only played nine games, because the first-place Bucs had played and won ten games.

Still, the Mets had a unique kind of momentum. In the first game, they'd gotten 13 hits and took a 2-1 lead in the fifth inning. It just seemed they couldn't ever get ahead to stay. The infield misplayed a series of balls in the seventh, turning Pittsburgh's three-run lead into six.

In the second game, the Mets led 2-0 through the top of the sixth, and Jim Hickman's seventh-inning single took a lucky hop, putting him in position to tie the score 3-3 when Chris Cannizzaro flied to left. Sadly for the Mets, Bill Mazeroski took the lead back in the eighth with a run-scoring triple.

Reviewing the Hitters

Casey Stengel had been an American Leaguer for 12 years before joining the Mets, and while his memory was excellent (when he wanted it to be), he was still getting used to the National League opposition. Stengel sent batting coach Rogers Hornsby to Cincinnati to scout the Reds, instead of accompanying the team to Pittsburgh. Stengel also leaned on some of his National League veterans for help, though always in his own unique way.

"Casey always wanted a meeting before, so we would go through the hitters," remembered Clem Labine. "All your traveling is done with these trunks, so we're all sitting on trunks in the clubhouse, waiting for Casey to come out from his office. He comes out with the scorecard in his hand. He looks around and looks around, and then he looks at me, and says, 'Hey! You're a National Leaguer, you know all these guys, here, go over the hitters.'

"So I thought, okay, well, fine. I sit down and I start, and I looked up, and he'd gone back into his office. He's gone! He didn't even come out! The manager has to be there, because we're talking about how you're going to pitch to these hitters. The manager is the guy who has to turn around and say, outfielder, get over this way. He's the guy with the last word. But this was Casey. It was the time in his life where things could be forgotten."

Identity Crisis

Casey Stengel never was good with names. He managed to mix up everyone, regardless of age, race, position, or team. One day, like a parent who calls her children by the name of the family pet, Stengel confused Sherman Jones, his 27-year-old, black right-handed pitcher, with Cookie Lavagetto, his 50-year-old, Italian coach.

"I was in the dugout, and Stengel walks up to me, walks past me, slaps me on the back, on the shoulder I think, and asks me a question," Jones recalled. "I forgot what the question was, but he called me Cookie. Joe Ginsberg was sitting beside me, I believe, and he said, 'Casey, that ain't Cookie.'

"Casey said, 'Aw, the hell. It looks just like him.'"

Stengel, left, with coach Cookie Lavagetto
DONALD UHRBROCK/TIME LIFE PICTURES/GETTY IMAGES

Close Games

The original Mets all make the same assertion: "We were in games." And they were. They played 58 one-run games and lost 39 of them, more than any other team that year.

"We were in a lot of ballgames," Rod Kanehl said. "And Casey always had a big bat to go to the plate. We went to bat with the tying run at the plate many times during that 62 season. He would have either (Marv) Throneberry to go up, or (Gene) Woodling, or Frank Thomas, or (Gil) Hodges, to pinch-hit with two outs in the ninth inning and the tying run on base. And they delivered at times, but not often enough."

No one likes losing, and the Mets never got used to it, not after nine losses in Pittsburgh in April and not after 90 losses in New York in August. It hurt every single time.

"It's not like they expected to lose every ballgame," Solly Hemus said. "They thought they could win every ball game. That's being a professional, being a competitor."

A Splitting Headache, Literally

In the first game at Pittsburgh, Bob Skinner knocked Met catcher Hobie Landrith in the head with his follow-through swing in the seventh inning. Landrith left the game for the hospital. He received eight stitches, Chris Cannizzaro moved into the starting lineup, and Landrith did not return to his post behind home plate until April 27.

Finally!

The Mets won their first major league game April 23, 1962, a 9-1 victory over Pittsburgh. Everyone shined. They even batted around in the second inning.

"That night, we jumped on them," Craig Anderson recalled. "Jay (Hook) was extremely sharp that night. Maybe the Pirates didn't think it was going to be that much of a game, and all of a sudden they're down six or seven runs."

Hook gave up five hits in nine innings and knocked in two runs with a single in the second. Elio Chacon played shortstop and had three hits. Felix Mantilla was back in the lineup, displacing the slumping Don Zimmer at third base, and he had three hits. The Mets tallied 14 hits overall, and for once their opponents' final lineup card was longer than theirs.

By the end of the Mets' first win, Casey Stengel was out of the dugout, jumping up and down and waving his arms. There was quite a bit of smiling and laughing in the Mets' clubhouse, welcome sights and sounds in what was becoming a generally depressing place.

Stengel was in top form. He vowed to pitch Jay Hook every day. He promised the team would win its next 99 games and contend for the pennant. It had not gone unnoticed, of course, that the 1961 Cincinnati Reds had survived an eight-game April losing streak, then won the pennant.

"I don't remember a whole lot about the game," Jay Hook said. "You just go out and figure you're going to do your best. But after the game, I went in, and of course all the writers were there, around my locker, and Casey had said to them, 'Take as much time as you want, we'll just hold up the bus, or the plane.'

"By the time we finished, the stadium had run out of hot water. So I took a bath in the whirlpool."

Walks Don't Always Help

The day after winning their first game, the Mets lost 7-3 to Cincinnati. Craig Anderson got knocked out after the first inning, in which he let the Reds get out to a 4-0 lead. The bad news is, the Mets drew 13 walks and needed every single one of them to score their three runs. Charlie Neal drove in one, and Mantilla two, and the walks stretched the game to just under four hours.

The Mets Make Trades

In assembling the Mets, George Weiss had wanted to put big names on the field. But he also wanted those big names to win ball games. And he was furiously working on trades, to get the team in order. Weiss's efforts reminded *Times* columnist Arthur Daley in mind of Bill Veeck, the owner of the perpetually miserable St. Louis Browns.

"I have three teams," Veeck said. "I have one coming, one going, and one on the field. If I can trade away enough Brownies to other teams, I can louse up the entire league."

Weiss seemed to be pursuing the same strategy. All general managers try to correct problems and make their teams better through trades, but to some of the Mets, it seemed excessive.

Salvation for Sammy Taylor

The day after the Mets lost No. 11, 7-1 in Cincinnati, they announced their first trade of the season. One month and one day before Bobby Gene (B.G.) Smith's 28th birthday, the Mets announced they were sending the little-used outfielder to Chicago for catcher Sammy Taylor. Smith had played in eight of the Mets' first games; in 22 at-bats, he had three hits.

On its face it seemed an even trade. Taylor had Smith-like statistics, but Weiss and the coaches hoped he might add some offensive heft to the Mets' catching rotation. The 29-year-old catcher had driven in 23 runs in 1961 and hit a career-best .269 for the Cubs just two years before that. Chicago would have liked to keep him, except that they had to suspend him. After playing seven games to start the season, Taylor decided that the Cubs weren't paying him enough to maintain houses in both Chicago and in his hometown of Woodruff, South Carolina, which his wife liked better than the Windy City. So Taylor moved to Woodruff and refused to play unless the Cubs traded him. Taylor might have returned to the Cubs if they'd offered him more money, but instead they suspended him.

When Taylor signed with the Mets, he wouldn't say how much he was getting paid, but allowed it was equivalent to his 1961 salary with the Cubs.

(Smith, it turned out, had a better year offensively than Taylor, but not by much. And besides, the Mets needed a catcher.)

Goodbye and Hello

Clem Labine and Joe Ginsberg were released and went home. Labine, the beloved Dodger pitcher, had pitched four innings of relief for the Mets, in which he amassed a 11.25 ERA. Ginsberg, a catcher, had gone hitless in five at-bats over the course of two games.

The Labine-Ginsberg release made room for Harry Chiti, a catcher in the Cleveland Indians farm system, and Dave Hillman, a right-handed pitcher from a minor-league team in Syracuse. Chiti, 29, had been up and down in the majors since 1950, and had only been an everyday player twice: in 1955 with Chicago, and in 1959 with Kansas City.

When Chiti got word that he'd been traded for a player to be named later, he told his wife Catherine, and it became the genesis of a long-standing joke between them. The Cleveland Indians had just hoisted their Chief Wahoo statue on top of the old Cleveland stadium. Catherine Chiti said it wasn't a good substitute for her husband, but it would have to do for the time being.

"I always laughed and said Wahoo belonged to me," Catherine Chiti recalled.

Dave Hillman, 34, was coming off a winning season in 1961, when he went 3-2 for the Boston Red Sox. Perhaps more relevant was his 21-37 career record, which included three full losing seasons with the Chicago Cubs.

Don't Call It a Comeback

The Mets returned home after their first road trip with a win under their belts. Now it was time to win one for the fans at the Polo Grounds. It didn't happen right away, as the Mets let the Phillies jump out to an 11-1 lead after five-and-a-half innings.

But the Mets never failed to make every game entertaining.

Down by 10 runs to the Phillies on April 27, Jim Marshall, Frank Thomas and Charlie Neal each scored in the bottom of the sixth. Hobie Landrith hit a run-scoring double in the eighth, and Ed Bouchee, pinch-hitting for reliever Herb Moford, followed up with a three-run homer to cut Philadelphia's lead to 11-8. One more run in the ninth inning brought the tying run to the plate—nearly hitless third-baseman Don Zimmer—with two outs. Zimmer struck out on a 3-2 pitch to end the game.

The King of Slumps

Don Zimmer was never an amazing hitter, but in his eight years in the major leagues, he'd never had this much trouble.

"I was great in spring training," Zimmer said. "And then I stunk up the joint."

Forty-two years later, Zimmer can and does laugh about that particularly disastrous April with the Mets.

"I was telling the guys in the [Yankees] coaches' room yesterday," Zimmer said in the early fall of 2003. "I got a hit the first day, I got a hit the second day, and then I went something like 0-for-28. And then I got a bloop hit and went 0-for-30-something again.

"You know, there is such a thing as hitting in tough luck, if you hit a good line drive and they catch it or something. I had them in the coaches' room laughing. I said to them, you hear of guys in tough luck, and they think I'm going to say that's what happened to me. They think I'm going to say I hit in tough luck.

"I told them, I didn't hit a ball good all spring."

Don Zimmer
DONALD UHRBROCK/TIME LIFE PICTURES/GETTY IMAGES

A Win at Home

The Mets' penchant for the late rally finally rewarded their home faithful with a win. On April 29, New York topped Philladelphia 8-6, after trailing by five runs heading into the second half of the sixth inning. Frank Thomas, Charlie Neal and Gil Hodges each hit home runs as the Mets scored six runs to take a 7-6 lead. Jim Hickman hit the final home run of the game in the bottom of the eighth. The nine homers by both teams combined tied a National League record at the time.

Lightning Strikes Twice

After their first win at home, the Mets won again the next day. Al Jackson shut out the Phillies, 8-0, in the first game of a doubleheader, and the Mets scored seven runs in a monstrous fourth inning. Frank Thomas tagged Art Mahaffey's first pitch for a home run to left field in the second; when Thomas faced Mahaffey in the fourth, the Phillies' pitcher hit Thomas in the foot. Thomas took his base, and on the next play, Philadelphia first baseman Roy Sievers hit Thomas in the back with a throw that was meant for the second baseman. Thomas scored on the next play, and came back up to bat later in the inning as the Mets batted around. This time Frank Sullivan hit Thomas on the arm, and the umpires went to the mound to talk to the pitcher.

"It's part of the game," Thomas said. "I just feel when the pitcher comes in close, he respects me, and I respect him for doing that, because he's protecting his plate."

Thomas became the second major leaguer to get hit by a pitch twice in the same inning, joining Willard Schmidt, a pitcher who earned that distinction during his 1959 season with the Cincinnati Reds. (Orioles outfielder Brady Anderson became the first player in the American League to join that exclusive club on May 23, 1999, when he was hit twice by Texas pitcher Mike Morgan in the first inning.)

Over Before It Began

The Mets didn't even get to sleep on their first winning streak. The Phillies rebounded and won the second game of the April 29 doubleheader 10-2. When that game was over, Al Jackson headed to the clubhouse to shower and change. The young pitcher expected to face the New York corps of sports reporters, who were, he supposed, waiting for him after his Game One triumph. He had never seen a media throng like these reporters, and with equal parts excitement and trepidation, Jackson dressed to face the writers.

They were nowhere to be found. It was a Sunday, Jackson recalled, and the crew covering the game was unusually light and eager to hustle out of the ballpark.

"I don't know if I was disappointed or relieved," he recalled.

Business Sense and Baseball, Too

Early in May, a New York businessmen's club gave Casey Stengel an award for being "baseball's top salesman of 1962." He joked around when he unwrapped the plaque, saying he had been searching for home plate.

"My players can't seem to find it," he said, according to the *New York Times*. "Now you can pick up the bases and the equipment, the bats and the balls from time to time, when you finish a game, but home plate is just supposed to sit there in the ground all day, and we can't seem to find it."

Stengel had endeared himself to the business community as well as baseball folks, because his business sense was as sharp as his baseball knowledge.

"People have asked me, is there anything that you learned from baseball that carried over into business," said Jay Hook. "And my answer was always yes. Casey knew who his customers were. His customers were the fans that were coming to the park and the fans that were watching these games on television. They created a market for the advertisers. And he knew that the vehicle to get to those fans was the sportswriters. So he did everything he could to make the sportswriters' job easier. I'll give you an example: If we had a rained-out game, the first thing Casey would do is get everybody a beer—all the writers—and call them in his office. They would sit there for two hours and talk about the team or talk about old times or talk about stories, so they'd have something to fill their columns with."

The Stengel Story Hour

Stengel entertained the players, too. Al Jackson recalled waiting around the locker room to see if the weather merited a delay or a cancellation. No one knew each other all that well yet, and so the players sat in front of their lockers, reading or talking quietly to their neighbors; it wasn't a particularly fun or even warm environment.

Then Casey Stengel walked in. He pulled a chair into the middle of the clubhouse, which wasn't that big to begin with, and he started talking. He wasn't talking to anyone in particular, and he didn't have a specific narrative to follow, he was just weaving yarns.

The players took notice. One by one, they pulled up on the floor to listen to the old man, turning the Mets' rain delay into story time.

"All 25 men were gathered around him like little kids," Jackson said. "It was something to see. I wish I had a picture of it."

A Nugget of Wisdom

The rain put the kibosh on all but one game in the Mets' home series with Cincinnati, which the Mets lost, 8-2. After pitching three scoreless innings, Jay Hook gave up five hits in a row in the fourth inning, putting the Mets in a 4-0 hole. Dave Hillman replaced him, one of four relievers yet to come.

Hook took the loss with him to the showers. After the game ended, he was standing at his locker talking with *New York Times* reporter Robert Lipsyte, who had written an article two weeks previously about the engineer-student pitcher explaining why a curve ball curves.

Casey Stengel walked in and saw the two of them talking.

"(Stengel) looks at me, then he looks back at Lipsyte," Hook said. "He looks back at me, looks back at Lipsyte, and then he said, 'You know, if Hook could only do what he knows.'"

Outnumbered

The Mets took the train to Philadelphia for a three-game series, and if outfielder John DeMerit had not yet grasped the importance of the Mets to New York's newspaper trade, it became clear to him on that trip.

"I think the train had one car for the ball club, and two for the writers if I remember it right," DeMerit said. "That was all new to me."

Two Down in Philly

The Mets lost their first two in Philadelphia. In both games, the Mets did plenty of things right and still managed to lose.

In the first game, the Mets scored three runs in the first inning, then Roger Craig walked the Phillies' lead-off man, gave up a home run, then a single, then walked another batter. Sherman Jones relieved him, though he didn't do much better, and the Mets' three-run lead shrunk to a one-run deficit by the end of the inning. Each time the Mets scored, the Phillies answered with a run of their own and stayed one run ahead of New York. In the ninth inning, with no outs and the bases loaded, the Mets failed to score and lost 6-5.

The next day, the Mets amassed seven hits and lost 2-1. Rod Kanehl, the tying run, was tagged out at home plate in the bottom of the ninth.

Just as He Was Heating Up

Don Zimmer broke through his hitless streak in the first game of the Philadelphia series. After the final game of the series, which the Mets won, 7-5, Casey Stengel told Zimmer, in a roundabout way, that he was being traded to the Cincinnati Reds.

"We came up the steps to the clubhouse that day, and I'll never forget it, we finally won a game," Zimmer said. "You know, we'd win one game, lose seven, win one, lose seven. When you won a game, you celebrated. We were coming up the steps and everybody's whooping and hollering, having a good time.

"I went into the shower, and there was no curtain or nothing, just an open shower. I could see Casey standing in the middle of the clubhouse. He had a towel wrapped around him, his sneakers on and those little bow legs sticking out. I saw him looking into the shower and I happened to look up and he gives me"—Zimmer winked and jerked his head—"you know, like, I want to see you. I finished my shower, got a towel and dried off. So I had a towel wrapped around me and the two of us were standing in the middle of the clubhouse and he said, 'You'll like it. The centerfield, you'll love it and I'm happy for you.'

"And he kept going on and on with his hands waving, and this and that, and centerfield you'll like it, you'll love it. I didn't know one thing he said yet. I was dumbfounded.

"Finally I said, 'Case, what are you trying to tell me?'

"'Oh,' he said. 'We just traded you to the Cincinnati Reds.'

"I don't know how long he was going to go on if I didn't stop him. What he meant by the center field was that it was a short ballpark—if you hit a ball 390 in center field, it was a home run in Crosley Field."

Was It Something About the Mets?

Leaving the Mets wasn't like leaving Chicago, where Zimmer was eager to get out of the zany system of rotating managers, but Zimmer was happy to head for Cincinnati, his hometown. His parents still lived there, and his father's health was declining.

"At that time, to be able to take my wife and two kids back to Cincinnati, there was really no better medicine for my mom and dad," Zimmer said. "That's what made it special for me."

He left the Mets with a grand total of four hits in 52 at-bats, including the one two games before he was traded. Stengel joked that he waited for Zimmer to get hot.

"The funny thing about it is I get traded to the Cincinnati Reds, and they know I'm 2-for-60 or whatever it was," Zimmer said. "The second night, (manager) Freddy Hutchinson looked at me and said, 'Go ahead, pinch hit.' And I got a hit.

"Two days later, he said, 'Pinch hit.' I think the first four times I went to bat for the Reds I got four hits. That was more than I got for the Mets in three weeks."

A Thumper for Third

Don Zimmer went to Cincinnati in exchange for Robert G. Miller, a left-handed pitcher, and Cliff Cook, a third baseman. At Indianapolis in 1961, Cook hit .311 with 35 home runs and 119 RBI and was named the Most Valuable Player of the minor league American Association. He hadn't fared quite as well in the major leagues; in his longest stint with the Reds, he hit .208 in 149 at-bats.

Cook looked promising. In his first game for the Mets, a 3-1 win in Chicago on May 8, he hit an infield single and made three nice plays at third base. The New York fans got a look at him at the beginning of the team's home series with Milwaukee three days later.

"I remember when we got Cliff Cook, he was supposed to be a pretty good thumper," said Bob Mandt. "He hit a triple, into left center field, a line drive as far as you could hit it, about 420 feet. And I thought, oh, man, our third base problems are over. Even then, third base was our headache. The only thing was, that night he made two assigned errors and maybe three more he should have been hit with. There were like five balls he should have had, and it just wasn't the answer."

Another Miller

Robert G. Miller was a left-handed reliever. He came to the Mets with 168 innings of big-league pitching experience since his first game with the Detroit Tigers in 1953. He too had spent most of the year in Indianapolis, where he'd gone 6-7 in relief.

Miller provided a doppelganger for the right-handed Bob Miller already on the Mets roster. To further complicate the issue, the right-handed Bob Miller's middle name was 'Lane,' so anyone hoping for a simple mnemonic—'L is for Lefty,' for example—was out of luck. The pair even became roommates. That way, if someone was looking for Bob Miller, at least they were sure to get the right room. The new Miller was already better than the old Miller, whose 0-2 record put him two games behind his new roommate.

And while everyone else confused the pair from time to time, Casey Stengel solved the problem in his own unique way: he always called left-handed Bob Miller "Nelson."

Robert G. Miller
BRACE PHOTO

Tell the Truth

The two Bob Millers had some fun with their circumstances and went on the TV game show, *To Tell the Truth*.

"When they said, 'Will the real Bob Miller please stand up?' we both stood up," Bob G. Miller told ESPN.com. "It was the first time that ever happened in the history of the show. People laughed so hard, it stopped the whole show. One of the panelists literally fell down backwards in his chair, he was laughing so hard."

Marshall Out, Mizell In

The same day the Mets got the second Bob Miller, they traded first baseman Jim Marshall to Pittsburgh for Wilmer (Vinegar Bend) Mizell, the left-handed pitcher who had bested the Mets in their first series at home. Mizell was two months shy of 32 when he joined New York, with 10 years of major league baseball experience and a career record of 89-85. He'd been an All-Star with the Cardinals in 1959, then helped the Pirates win the world series in 1960.

Mizell suffered from a case of false advertising, both in name and reputation. First of all, he wasn't from Vinegar Bend, Alabama; he was from Leakesville, Mississippi, which was across the Escatawpa River and the state line. Vinegar Bend was just the nearest town with a post office.

The Arrival of Marvin Eugene Throneberry

On May 9, the Mets cancelled their game with Chicago because of the weather, sent Sherman Jones (0-4) to Syracuse, and bought Marvin Throneberry from the Baltimore Orioles. Throneberry, a 27-year-old first baseman, had played his best baseball in the Yankees' farm system, where he hit 82 home runs and knocked in 269 RBI over 1956 and 57. He had played semi-regularly in the Bronx in '58 and '59, then was sent to the Kansas City Royals in a seven-player trade that brought Roger Maris to the Yankees.

Since then, Throneberry had never quite achieved the same notoriety. But that didn't last long.

Ninth!

All the trading and the promise of new talent seemed to do the Mets good. They beat the Cubs 3-1 in Chicago, pushing their hosts into 10th place and happily taking over ninth. Jay Hook pitched a complete-game four-hitter, and improved his record to 2-1.

When the team's plane landed at LaGuardia Airport, Casey Stengel told his players, "Fix your ties, fellers, we're now in ninth place."

Anderson Wins Two

Revamped and rejuvenated, the Mets swept their doubleheader with the Braves on May 12. After fielding an entirely right-handed lineup against the lefty Warren Spahn,

Casey Stengel sent left-handed catcher Hobie Landrith to pinch-hit in the bottom of the ninth, with a runner on and two outs. Landrith hit a home run to right field to win the game, 3-2. Gil Hodges won the second game the same way, with a home run to right field in the bottom of the ninth that handed the Mets the 8-7 win.

Craig Anderson closed both games and earned both wins. In the first, he relieved Roger Craig after the old Dodger put in seven innings of work; in the second, Anderson was the last of six Met pitchers to take the mound, relieving Vinegar Bend Mizell, who faced one batter and walked him in his debut for the Mets.

Craig Anderson
BRACE PHOTO

Don't Spend It All in One Place

The doubleheader with Milwaukee was the first of three doubleheaders the Mets won in 1962, which was good for the records, but put the New York fans in a fix.

"Rarely did you see them win," said Jack Lang. "They won three doubleheaders, so that was six of their wins in three days, that only left 34 other days to see them win. There was a younger generation of fans that went to the ball-park not to see the Mets win but to see how they made fools of themselves today. They were dubbed by *Daily News* columnist Dick Young as 'The New Breed.' They were younger fans than had been Dodger and Giant fans in the old days, and the new fans were more rousing, they enjoyed having a lot of fun at the ballpark, whereas the old fans wanted to see the Mets win."

Chacon's Streak

Elio Chacon put together a nice little hitting streak during the Mets' doubleheader with the Braves. He reached base in seven straight at-bats, with five hits and two walks (he went three-for-three in the second game). For his streak to last, he would have had to be playing for a different team.

He came to the plate in the first inning of the fourth and final game of the series and promptly struck out. The Braves won that game 3-2.

Beating Chicago

May was turning into a decent month for the Mets, or so it seemed. A split with the Braves gave way to two wins at home against Chicago, both, by the same score, 6-5, in extra innings.

Chicago was prone to its own Met-like moments. In fact, the Cubs and the Mets were battling each other to stay out of the cellar. New York got ahead in the first game, when Barney Schultz, Chicago's fifth pitcher, walked Hobie Landrith with the bases loaded to lose it for Chicago in the 13th inning. The game ended at 1 a.m.

Less than 24 hours later, Felix Mantilla hit a bases-loaded single in the 11th to finish the second game. The Mets' record was 9-18: they were safely in ninth.

Worth the $50

In the first game of the Mets' four-game series at Milwaukee, Warren Spahn drilled opposing pitcher Roger Craig in the back in the third inning. Craig responded by throwing at Spahn's head two innings later, at which point both pitchers were warned and fined $50. Why did the umpire wait until Craig retaliated to warn Spahn?

"Maybe he called the fine on Roger because he missed me," Spahn joked to reporters the next day. "I, at least, hit him."

Three Squeakers

The Mets finished their series in Milwaukee with three straight wins. In the first, the Mets mounted an eighth-inning rally that erased the Braves' three-run lead. Ken MacKenzie earned the win, after pitching the sixth and seventh inning, but Craig Anderson pitched two hitless innings to hold on to the 6-5 win.

They won the next day's doubleheader with late-inning onslaughts, erasing a four-run deficit in the first game, and snapping a tie in the second.

A Long Journey South

The three wins at Milwaukee comprised the Mets' longest winning streak and sent them hurtling into eighth place. They had won nine of their last 12 and were feeling good as they headed for the airport to fly to Houston.

"We were celebrating in Milwaukee," recalled Anderson, who also closed the first game of the doubleheader. "They took us to the bowling alley, and we were in the bowling alley for hours, bowling, and actually enjoying ourselves."

Their good moods couldn't even be spoiled by the fact that their flight out of Milwaukee was delayed for two hours. Once in the air, fog and mist over Houston forced the plane to land in Dallas, where the Mets waited another two hours.

That bizarre twist made the exceedingly long journey entirely futile for hitting coach Rogers Hornsby. He had spent the previous two weeks scouting prospects in Texas, then left Dallas early on the morning of May 20, watched the Mets win their doubleheader, then found himself back in Dallas exactly 24 hours later.

They finally arrived in Houston just in time for rush hour and fought traffic on the way to their hotel. On his way up to his room at 8 a.m., Casey Stengel said, "If anyone wants me, tell 'em I'm being embalmed."

Chapter
8

THE LOSING
STREAK

Losing Two in Texas

The Mets failed to beat Houston, the other expansion club, in New York, and they couldn't do it on their first trip to Texas, either. After winning three in a row in Milwaukee, then flying overnight, the Mets promptly dropped two games to Houston, both by the score of 3-2, both with big eighth-inning game-winning hits by the Colt .45s.

Jet Lag

The travel was starting to wear on the team. To get to Los Angeles from Houston, the team flew out after the last night game in the series, only to land in LA at 5:45 the next morning, with a game that night. Roger Craig, the starter in LA, had flown out the day before, so he could be well rested for the series opener.

The extra rest helped Craig: he held the Dodgers to one run, which the Mets matched, through the seventh inning.

But a Richie Ashburn error featured in the Dodgers' two-run rally in the eighth and Don Drysdale held the Mets to four hits.

For the third night in a row, the Mets had lost a tied ballgame in the eighth inning. No wonder Casey Stengel was dying for a pitcher to go nine innings: in their last three games, the Mets hadn't had to pitch the bottom of the ninth.

Coffee, Tea, or Frank Thomas

On that trip west, Frank Thomas let it be known that he was good at more than just baseball. As soon as the Mets' flights took off, Thomas would get up out of his seat and head to the plane's galley, where he instructed the stewardesses, "You get the meals ready, I'll deliver them and bring them back to you."

"The reason why I did that was because I knew how hungry the players were," Thomas said. "I really enjoyed helping them and getting the players their food fast, because I knew they were hungry."

He brought meals to the reporters who traveled on the team's flights, too, and he was serious with everyone. According to one account, when a reporter waved off Thomas on account of the reporter was winning at cards, Thomas said, "Fine, but you eat last." When the card game was over, the reporter asked one of the stewardesses for a meal, and she brought it to him. Thomas was irate when he found out the reporter had gone behind his back.

Frank Thomas
BRACE PHOTO

Say Hey

The Mets' game at San Fransisco's Candlestick Park on May 26 marked the two clubs' first meeting of the season, and therefore, the first time the current denizens of the Polo Grounds played the storied former residents.

Giants fans were angry when their team left New York in 1957, but they didn't seem to stay quite as bitter for quite as long as Dodgers fans. They hated owner Horace Stoneham, of course, but Willie Mays remained a beloved player in the city. Mrs. Payson had been a Giants fan all her life, and she flew to San Fransisco for the team's inaugural game on the West Coast. She tried several times to buy Mays for the Mets, and she wasn't the only one who wanted to see him in New York. (The New York faithful eventually got their wish. The Giants traded Mays to the Mets in 1972, and the Hall of Famer played the last two years of his career in New York.) It was often said that the Mets fans' ideal game was one in which Mays hit four home runs, and the Mets won 5-4.

Mays did hit a couple home runs, but his first wiped out the Mets' one-run lead, and his second one won the game for the Giants 7-6 in the tenth inning.

"Willie was the only player I ever saw where he was so good, the other players on his team couldn't help but watch him," Al Jackson said.

The Mets on the Town

In spite of all the losing, road trips were proving to be a pretty good time for the Mets. They took the opportunity to shop and sightsee. Once on a trip to San Francisco, Ken Mackenzie bought an electric train set for his son, then came back to the hotel, where he shared a room with Vinegar Bend Mizell. The two pitchers set up the train in their room.

"Mizell was on the floor, watching the train like a little kid," Mackenzie recalled.

The challenge of travel, Rod Kanehl said, was having fun on the Mets' small daily allowance.

"We'd go into Los Angeles, and we'd stay downtown at the Hilton, and all the action was up in Hollywood," Kanehl said. "Well, the cab ride was $6 one way. The cabs in LA are atrocious. You'd spend your daily meal money on cabs. You'd go to San Francisco at the start of a 10-day road trip or a 12-day road trip, and they'd give you the cash the first day. They'd give you $120. After four, five days, you're borrowing from your friend or the traveling secretary. You just can't go into San Francisco on $12 a day."

Mays's First Fight

Before they ended their first series in San Fransisco, the Mets managed to help make history one more time: they incited Willie Mays to his first fight.

The opening game of the May 27 double header started to get tense in the top of the seventh inning when Giants first baseman Orlando Cepeda knocked Mets outfielder Joe Christopher out of the game. Trying to turn a double play, Cepeda threw to second base and beaned Christopher on the basepath. The right fielder was still wearing his batting helmet and wasn't seriously hurt, but he had to leave the game.

In the bottom of the seventh, Mays tagged Roger Craig for a run-scoring single and a 4-1 San Fransisco lead. Cepeda came to bat next, and Craig hit him in the back. Cepeda looked as though he might rush the mound, then headed for first base, then charged back toward Craig. San Fransisco manager Alvin Dark came out of the dugout, grabbed his first baseman and returned him to first base.

Craig wouldn't leave Cepeda alone and tried to pick him off first. He almost had him, too, but first baseman Ed Bouchee couldn't hold on to the throw. Then Craig turned and tried to pick Mays off second base. Mays slid safely back into the base, feet first.

The next thing you knew, Elio Chacon, the 160-pound, 5-foot-9 second baseman, was punching at Willie Mays. The centerfielder, who had a dozen pounds and a couple inches on Chacon, picked up the Mets' second baseman and threw him to the ground. Cepeda took advantage of the confusion to head back toward the pitchers mound.

Rod Kanehl was playing third base, and watched the melee with San Fransisco's Jim Davenport.

"Jim and I had played some minor league ball against each other back in '55, '56, and we'd known each other a long time," Kanehl said. "And when the fight broke out, he started to run, and I grabbed him. I said, 'Hey, this thing is bigger than the both of us. Let's just watch.'

"Chacon got thrown out of the game, and I ended up playing shortstop. I think it was the only time I played shortstop in the big leagues."

Chacon insisted Mays had spiked him and in fact that Mays spiked him every time he could. The umpires ejected Chacon and fined him $100.

The second game was less eventful, except for the eighth inning, in which the Mets gave back their three-run lead and lost the game, 6-5.

That marked the end of their road trip, and the Mets returned to New York on an eight-game losing streak. The good news was they were going home. The bad news was that the Giants and the Dodgers were coming with them.

New York Welcomes the Dodgers and the Giants

For the first time since 1957, the Dodgers returned to the Polo Grounds, to open a five-day, seven-game baseball smorgasbord that also featured those other New York exiles, the Giants.

"That was a high moment of 1962," said Bob Mandt. "Where we didn't quite sell out the place every day, but I bet it was 40 percent of our attendance the entire year. We got swept, we lost all the games. But in doing so, we had some records that stood for quite a while, as far as attendance records. Biggest Sunday, biggest Friday night, biggest double-header, things like that. They held up for a long time. So there were some pluses. But losing every game, against the Dodgers and Giants, that hurt."

More than 55,000 people turned out on the first day of the Dodgers series, and they saw Gil Hodges hit three home runs over the course of the two games, bringing his career total to 369, which tied him with Mets announcer and former Pittsburgh Pirate Ralph Kiner at tenth on the all-time list. They also saw the Mets turn a triple play—Chacon to Mantilla to Hodges—to stave off a Dodger rally in the second game, which they lost by a run in the ninth inning anyway.

At the time, Sandy Koufax called it the most exciting game he'd ever pitched.

"Maybe it was just being back in the big town again," he told the *Times*. "I was higher than a kite. It was an emotional jag and I couldn't relax. That crowd was unbelievable and it added to the excitement. It was such an enthusiastic crowd, and it never stopped cheering for the Mets, no matter how hopelessly out of it they were. That's what startled us so much. We never expected the fans to cheer for the Dodgers—some might be a little bit mad at our leaving—but we were surprised that the Mets could get and hold such a following so fast."

The fans were perhaps the most notable thing about the Memorial Day weekend games. The team sold 197,433 tickets for the five-day series, more than doubling the season's attendance. And the fans' exuberance could not be quantified. After Felix Mantilla hit a home run in the seventh inning of the opener with the Giants, a fan ran into the Mets' dugout, and the game had to be stopped while he was removed. The next day, as the Mets lost both ends of a doubleheader, six Met fans were arrested for disorderly conduct.

It didn't seem to bother anyone in the bleachers that, by the end of the series, the Mets had lost 15 in a row.

They Couldn't Buy a Win

The Mets opened their early June road trip with a doubleheader in Philadelphia. They lost both games. It could have been worse. They could have lost three, but they'd been rained out of the series' first game the day before.

The Mets were shut out in the first game for the first time that season, but the second loss was the worse of the two, partly because Al Jackson took a 1-0 lead into the eighth inning, then gave up a solo home run to Tony Taylor. Craig Anderson relieved Jackson in the bottom of the ninth, then gave up the winning hit on his first pitch.

The 2-1 loss in the second game extended the Mets' losing streak to 17 games. It wasn't the worst ever: the Phillies owned that record, after dropping 23 straight in 1961. But it was the worst ever for a New York baseball team, surpassing the 1944 Brooklyn Dodgers' 16-game losing streak.

Say Goodbye to Landrith

The Mets were full of surprises in early June. When they had brought Marv Throneberry to the team three weeks previously, they announced that the deal had been done for cash. No one heard them mention a player to be named later, but on June 7, they named one. The Mets announced they were sending catcher Hobie Landrith, who had been their first pick in the expansion draft, to the Orioles to complete the Throneberry trade.

The Landrith announcement raised expectations for the new first baseman. Mets fans had thought they had gotten him for free—or at least, without having to give anything up other than cash. Now it turned out they were losing a decent catcher. Landrith was hitting .289 and only had three passed balls.

Marv Throneberry turned out to be worth it. Even from a baseball standpoint, the deal was a good one, as Landrith's hitting and catching both suffered in Baltimore.

Marv Throneberry
AP/WWP

Relief at Long Last

After losing 17 straight, there was some good news. The Cubs, the second-worst team of 1962, were coming to town. On June 8, Chicago helped the Mets out of their jam. Jim Hickman hit a single to open the ninth inning, and the Mets loaded the bases on two Chicago errors. Elio Chacon struck out, and it seemed the Mets were doomed to another almost-but-not-quite finish. Charlie Neal saved the day with a sacrifice fly to right field that gave the Mets a 4-3 lead. Craig Anderson held the Cubs scoreless in the bottom of the ninth for the Mets' first win in 16 days.

Their winning streak ended at one, however. The Cubs won the second half of the doubleheader.

Chapter
9

THE SEASON
CONTINUES

Defender of the Meals

The Mets traveled back to Houston for a three-game series played in the excessive heat of a Texas June. Al Jackson succeeded in pitching New York to its first win against the other expansion team—3-1 in the first game of the series—and Frank Thomas, outfielder and team flight attendant, got into a row with trainer Gus Mauch over the plane's meals.

When the team's charter plane had arrived in Houston, more than a dozen of the meals were destroyed during a particularly hard landing. Thomas insisted that, if there weren't enough meals to go around, that the players would eat and the writers would go without. Mauch wanted the writers to get their meals. The conversation got quite heated, and Thomas won the argument.

"Frank was right in the middle of that," Craig Anderson said. "But he was right on that one."

Traded for Himself

At the beginning of June, the Harry Chiti trade was completed, an action that inscribed the catcher into the annals of baseball trivia forever. He had come to the Mets at the end of April, for the ubiquitous "player to be named later." June 15 was later and the Indians wanted their player. They got him. The Mets sent Chiti back to the Cleveland system, trading him, in effect, for himself.

It didn't take a great toll on Chiti. His family was still in the Cleveland area; he hadn't been in New York long enough for them to move.

"I had never gone to New York, because the kids were in school," Catherine Chiti, Harry's wife, recalled. "In fact, I was packed and ready to go to New York, when he called and said he'd been sent back to Cleveland."

Harry Chiti may be the most famous player to be traded for himself, but he isn't the only one. Clint (Scrap Iron) Courtney, the first catcher to wear glasses, was traded by, and returned to, the Baltimore Orioles during the 1961 off season.

That Fateful Father's Day

Many of the Mets had children, and some of the Mets had many children (Frank Thomas and Richie Ashburn could have fielded a lineup with their progeny alone). That didn't sanctify Father's Day, though, which evolved into perhaps the most infamous day of the season.

The Mets had a doubleheader with the Cubs, against whom the Mets had managed some success that season. There was no reason to think they couldn't win at least one of the two.

Marv Throneberry gave them a reason, though nothing went right from the beginning. Al Jackson walked the first batter of the first inning, Don Landrum, who tried to steal second while the next batter struck out. The Mets caught him in a rundown, and Landrum headed back to first. He found Throneberry in the basepath—what athletes like to call a mental error—which was the best thing that could have happened to Landrum, who ran smack into Throneberry and went safely to second base on the interference call. Instead of two out and none on, the Cubs now had one out, a man in scoring position, and their third, fourth and fifth hitters up to bat. Ron Santo hit a two-run triple. And then Lou Brock did something that was certainly not the Mets' fault: he hit a home run into the right centerfield bleachers, 460 feet from home plate.

No one had ever hit one into the right centerfield bleachers before, at least, not during a major league game. The ball sailed right over the heads of the Mets relievers in the bullpen.

"It was a high, high fly ball," Craig Anderson said. "It bounced off the board and into the bleachers."

Throneberry's error and Brock's bit of history put the Mets behind 4-0 at the end of the Cubs' half of the first inning. Throneberry nearly redeemed himself in the bottom of the inning, when he hit a deep triple to right field, scoring two runners. Throneberry watched from third base as the Cubs threw the ball to second and the umpire called Throneberry out for missing the bag.

Casey Stengel came out of the dugout to make his case.

In one version of the story, coach Cookie Lavagetto restrained Stengel at the dugout steps, saying, "I wouldn't argue too much, Casey, he missed first base too."

Solly Hemus said Stengel made it to the field to argue:

"He ran out to second base. And the umpire, he says, 'If they throw to first base, you're not going to get any runs at all.' So Casey just turned right around and went back to the dugout."

In a third version, instead of retiring quietly to the dugout, Stengel made one last effort: "Well," he yelled, "I know he didn't miss third base, because he's standing right on it!"

And in a fourth version, it was Throneberry himself who argued the call.

"Tell them I touched second, Casey," he said to his manager.

"I would," Stengel replied, "but you didn't touch first either."

Following Instructions

Jay Hook was on the mound for a June 18 start against the Braves when Hank Aaron came up to bat in the third inning with the bases loaded. Casey Stengel ventured to the mound to give his pitcher, whom Stengel called 'Professor' on account of his graduate work in engineering, some advice.

"Professor," Stengel said, "pitch him outside and make him hit it to centerfield."

This was the usual practice for pitching to home-run hitters in the Polo Grounds. While the foul poles were short, only two batters had ever homered to the center field bleachers: one, Joe Adcock, who was in the Braves' lineup June 18, had done it nine years previously; the Cubs' Lou Brock had done it the day before. Twice in 40-some years? Those seemed like pretty good odds, so Hook followed instructions.

"Well, the next pitch I threw was a fastball," Hook said. "And Aaron hit it about 600 feet to centerfield, for a grand-slam home run. Needless to say, I was out of the game after that pitch."

Craig Anderson saw it all from the bullpen.

"Brock's was a high fly, but Aaron's was a line shot," Anderson said. "It was an unusual circumstance."

In another unfortunate turn of events for the Mets, Gus Bell, whom the Mets had left with the Braves a month previously to complete the Frank Thomas trade, played wonderfully against his old team. His batting average had improved 174 points in the month since he'd joined the Braves, and he hit a triple, then scored, to give Milwaukee a lead in the top of the second inning. He also stifled a Mets rally with a running catch deep in left field in the bottom of the same.

Finally Beating Houston

The Mets logged a second win against Houston, the other expansion team, on June 22, when Al Jackson pitched his second shutout in the first game of a doubleheader, which the Mets won 2-0. He ruined his no-hitter in the first inning, when he gave up a single to Joey Amalfitano. He walked the next batter, but then retired the rest of the Colts.

Too bad Jackson couldn't pitch the second one, too: the Mets lost 16-3 in a game tarnished by six Met errors. The score was only 11-3 heading into the last inning, but Marv Throneberry made his third error of the game as Houston scored five in the ninth.

A Foregone Term in a Bygone Era

Occasionally throughout the season, players hit what the sportswriters called an "Oriental" home run. The term referred to the short home runs, or the "ground rule" home runs that bounced off outfield overhangs.

"It meant cheap," said *Newsday* columnist Stan Isaacs. "Oriental goods in the old days, long before Japan and China became powerful, they were considered cheap, things were made in Japan and China and sold here. So if a home run was cheap, it was considered an Oriental home run. ... It was a racist term. You never would have seen it in *Newsday*, or the *Times*."

In fact, most papers used the phrase. While it would be considered unacceptable by 21st-century standards, it was widely used in the 1960s.

The Dodgers Deserved It

The Mets had a losing record against every other team in the National League except Chicago, with whom New York managed an even split. The worst futility the Mets faced, however, was against Pittsburgh and the Dodgers. The Mets' first win at Pittsburgh was one of two New York mustered against the Bucs, and New York also lost 14 of 16 to the Dodgers.

Jay Hook won one of those games against the Dodgers late in June, though it is probably more accurate to say the Dodgers lost it. Three Los Angeles pitchers issued seven walks—and consequently, four runs—to the Mets in the first inning. By the time the game was over, the Mets had scored 10 runs on four hits, and walked 16 times. It wasn't a record, though: in 1944, the Dodgers (then Brooklyn) had walked the Giants 17 times.

But the Mets couldn't count on the Dodgers to beat themselves every night. On June 30, Sandy Koufax pitched his first no-hitter, the first of the National League season. He struck out the first three Mets on nine pitches, and went on to strike out 10 more before the end of the game.

Not This Bonus Baby

One way to avoid the disappointment of losing was to leave early, which is what Casey Stengel did during a four-game series at San Francisco. The Mets were losing 5-1 in the fourth inning when Stengel headed for the exit. The Associated Press later confirmed that he had gone 80 miles to Stockton, California, to visit Bob Garibaldi. Stengel traveled to the 19-year-old right-hander's home town to try to convince him to join the Mets.

Meanwhile, the Mets lost 10-1 to the Giants.

Garibaldi turned Stengel down and signed with San Francisco for $135,000. Twelve days later, Garibaldi made his major league debut in the Polo Grounds, where he retired the Mets in order in the eighth inning.

The Mets, however, did everything they could to give him second thoughts and handed the Giants their first loss in the Polo Grounds since 1957.

Hodges's Landmark, Kanehl's Second Billing

Pitcher Bobby Shantz was an old friend of Rod Kanehl's. The two had lived out at Madeira Beach in St. Petersburg during Yankee spring training in 1959, and they had carpooled to the field every day with neighbors Ralph Houk and Gil McDougald.

On July 6, Kanehl and Shantz, then pitching for St. Louis, reconnected during a game at the Polo Grounds. Kanehl, who had replaced Frank Thomas in left field late in the game, hit the team's first grand-slam home run in the eighth inning.

Mrs. Payson, back from Europe, applauded and cheered the 10-3 win from the stands. Under other circumstances, such a hit would have made Kanehl the hero of the day, and in front of the owner, no less. But in the second inning, Gil Hodges hit his 370th career home run, placing him tenth on the all-time list, and first among National League right-handers.

"The headline on the sports pages was, 'Hodges hits 370' and in little print underneath, it said 'Kanehl hits grand slam,'" Kanehl recalled.

It was the first grand-slam of Kanehl's career.

"I just got up there and hit what I saw," he said. "If a ground ball's hit to you, you just pick it up and throw it. There wasn't anything scientific about baseball in those days."

The Origins of Marvelous Marv

Marv Throneberry was slowly becoming a notable Met. He could swing the bat, for one thing. For another, he had what the players joked were "iron wrists," that is to say, his defense didn't quite hold up his offense.

Before the Mets' July 7 doubleheader with St. Louis, Throneberry decided to take his reputation into his own hands. He found pitcher Jay Hook in the clubhouse.

"Hook, you're an engineer, aren't you?" Throneberry asked.

Hook allowed that he was.

"Well, engineers can print real good, can't they?" Throneberry said.

Hook said yes, he'd taken drafting classes and he supposed he could print well enough. So Throneberry took his nameplate down from above his locker, handed it to Hook, and said, "Write 'Marvelous Marv.'"

"He just probably thought that would be fun to do," said Hook. "I have no idea of his rationale, other than being a prankster, or thinking it'd be fun. So I printed it, and he put it above his locker."

In the opener that day, Throneberry pinch-hit a two-run homer in the ninth inning to lead the Mets over the Cardinals 5-4. He then hit a home run and a ninth-inning, two-out triple in the second game. Gene Woodling struck out to leave Throneberry in position to tie the game, but that wasn't Throneberry's fault.

After the game, Hook witnessed the birth of a legend.

"You know how all these writers are after a game, they come up by your locker," Hook said. "They were all at Marv's locker, and the next day, there it was, in the headlines, 'Marvelous Marv'."

When the Baseball Writers Association of America presented Throneberry with the Ben Epstein "Good Guy" award, Dick Young wrote this about the first baseman's nickname:

"If his first name had been Terrence, they'd have called him 'Terrible Terry,' but it was Marvin, and what alliterative sportswriter would call a man 'Terrible Marv,' even if it was a fact?

"So Marvelous Marv it was—in print, and in the spoken word. And always in jest."

Stan the Man Takes New York

For the second time in his career, Stan Musial hit three home runs in a game, a 15-1 defeat of the Mets at the Polo Grounds on July 8. The Mets didn't hit any.

Maybe it was something about New York. The last time Musial hit three in a game, it was May 2, 1954, and the Giants (then New York) were visiting St. Louis.

1951 All Over Again

Just because the Mets were less than a year old didn't mean they couldn't have an old-timers' day. The truth was, George Weiss (something of an old-timer himself) liked the reunions, so he brought some old New York players back for the Mets' first ever old-timers' game. No one cared that they weren't actually Mets, especially when they were the 1951 Dodgers and Giants.

The rematch of the Giants' Bobby Thomson and Dodgers pitcher Ralph Branca generated quite a bit of anticipation. Thomson, of course, hit a three-run homer off Branca in the bottom of the ninth inning of the third game of a three-game playoff series for the National League pennant. By the time the Mets reunited the two, it was clear Branca wasn't happy with his infamy. He quoted Shakespeare.

"The good that men do is oft interred with their bones and the evil lives on," Branca told reporters.

First the pitcher had said he wouldn't come. Then he said he wouldn't pitch. Perhaps looking for an exhibition game's worth of redemption, Branca came to the mound. Thomson came to the plate. A light rain began to fall. Branca threw two balls and two strikes and on the fifth pitch, Thomson hit to center field. Duke Snider made the catch — then, to perfectly torture Branca, he threw the ball over the roof in the infield.

The exhibition game and Branca's on-field misery over, the Mets' struggles began. Even Richie Ashburn's sixth home run of the season, more than he'd ever hit before, couldn't make a dent for the Mets, who lost for the third time in a row to the Dodgers, 17-3.

Who's Catching?

In the middle of July, the Mets bought catcher Joe Pignatano from the Giants for cash. He was less than a month from his 33rd birthday and playing his sixth season of major league baseball. He hadn't played particularly consistently in the previous five. You could call him more of an every-other-day player—he hit in the low .200s and averaged a handful of passed balls and errors every season. Some ex-Dodger fans no doubt recognized him as the rookie pinch runner who tried to steal an occupied base in 1957.

Eager to make a good impression on his new ball club, Pignatano came early to his first game at the Polo Grounds. He put on his new uniform and went out to the field. He saw Casey Stengel in the dugout and, without trying to be too obvious about it, sat down near his new manager. Soon the two were talking about all sorts of baseball-related matters, including the club's various problems. Game time was fast approaching, and, according to Pignatano's account in a 1968 article in the *Sunday News*, Jack Lang approached the dugout.

"Who's catching today?" Lang asked Stengel.

"Pignatano," Stengel replied. "If he ever gets here."

Get Well Gil

Gil Hodges, who had become the National League's leading career home run hitter earlier in the season, entered Roosevelt Hospital in the middle of July to have kidney stones removed. He was in the hospital for three weeks, and though he returned to the Mets' lineup in September, he was never seemed back to full strength. His teammates thought his knee trouble was also getting worse.

"I remember Gil Hodges getting off the bus," recalled Frank Thomas. "He was sitting in the front seat, and he got up, and he put his foot down, and his knee buckled."

Hodges played after that incident, Thomas said, but he never played very much. It was clear his playing days were coming to a hasty close.

Who, Me?

Felix Mantilla recalled that Casey Stengel never seemed to keep anyone's name straight. Once, after Mantilla had played a full game, Stengel subbed for his infielder as the game went into extra innings. Soon enough, Stengel was pacing the dugout, looking for a big bat to go to the plate.

Stengel strode up to Mantilla.

"Go pinch hit," he told him.

"Pinch hit," Mantilla said incredulously. "I just played the whole game!"

Felix Mantilla
BRACE PHOTO

The Writing on the Wall

The Mets commenced their second-longest losing streak of the season July 15. They dropped the second game of a doubleheader with the Giants, and didn't win again until July 27. During that 11-game losing streak, the Mets gained and lost the lead in four consecutive games. By the time the Mets lost the final game of the streak—Warren Spahn pitched his 319th career win as the Braves topped New York 6-1—the New York team was 23-73. *New York Times* reporter-cum-fortune-teller Gordon White wrote: "(The Mets) seem intent on establishing a major modern mark for defeats in a season."

The Marv Throneberry Fan Club

Marv Throneberry further solidified his reputation as the Met fans hated to love. First of all, the press had realized that Marvin Eugene Throneberry was not only a Met in uniform, he was born a M.E.T. as well. *Newsday* columnist Stan Isaacs thought there was just too much poetry in Throneberry, and named himself the president of the Marv Throneberry fan club.

"It just struck me, that fans are so much down on him, that it really would be something if somehow it was turned around," Isaacs said. "So I came up with a concept—the opposite side of hate is love—so they're hating him so much that somehow this could be turned into love. Somehow that's what happened. He was so bad, he became good, if you can understand that kind of craziness."

Throneberry wasn't immediately ready for the attention. He had just gotten used to the booing. More than once Throneberry heard the fans booing one of his teammates and quipped, "Hey, you're stealing my fans." When Isaacs and the other writers championed Throneberry, the first baseman had to get used to his minor celebrity.

"It took him a while to understand it," Isaacs said. "He was used to booing and all that, and now it was changing, so he was a little puzzled. He saw what was happening, that people were liking him, and he had a couple of good moments, so it all worked to help him become an endearing figure."

On July 21, Throneberry offered more encouragement to his fan club. The Mets led Cincinnati 3-2 in the fifth inning, and with two out, Don Blasingame hit a ground ball to first base. Instead of making the easy out to end the inning, Throneberry bobbled the ball. Blasingame was safe, and the next batter, Vada Pinson, hit a home run that gave the Reds the lead for good.

I Wouldn't Want Him Mad at Me

None of the Mets liked losing. Richie Ashburn really hated it, and he frequently took it out on the umpires. Ashburn thought he recognized a circular logic working against his team: because they were losing, they didn't get calls, and not getting calls made it that much harder to win, and therefore earn the benefit of the umpires' doubt. So he let the referees know when he thought they'd missed a call. Sometimes it came back to haunt the outfielder.

Once Ashburn tried to convince Casey Stengel to play him at catcher, a position Ashburn had played occasionally in the minor leagues. According to the *Sporting News*, Stengel said absolutely not.

"Imagine if I put him in there and he let one get by and it hit the umpire in the belly?" Stengel said. "They would have lynched me. They would have said he did it on purpose, to get even with those umpires. You know, the way he gets on them, it's a wonder he gets all those walks."

Gil Hodges saw an ejection waiting to happen and bet Ashburn $100 that he'd get himself thrown out sooner or later. Hodges won his bet July 22, when Ashburn teed off on umpire Vinnie Smith in the first game of a doubleheader with Cincinnati. According to *Newsday*, Stengel went out to talk to Smith.

"What did you say to make him so mad?" Stengel asked Smith.

"I didn't say anything," Smith said. "He said everything."

Hodges was still in the hospital, but when he got wind of the incident, he called Frank Thomas and told him to remind Ashburn of their bet. That set Ashburn off all over again.

Confusion in Any Language

Richie Ashburn was tired of chasing fly balls only to run into Venezuelan shortstop Elio Chacon. Ashburn figured the confusion was linguistic, and asked bilingual outfielder Joe Christopher how to say "I've got it" in Spanish.

Christopher taught Ashburn to say "Yo la tengo," and Ashburn practiced dutifully. The next time a hitter popped up to shallow centerfield, Ashburn yelled, "Yo la tengo! Yo la tengo!" Chacon promptly pulled up.

Ashburn prepared to make the catch, only to be bowled over by the English-speaking leftfielder Frank Thomas.

The Eli

Ken MacKenzie received a visit from Casey Stengel on the pitcher's mound one day. Stengel famously told the pitcher, a Yale graduate, "Make like they're the Harvards."

"What most people don't realize, is that Casey knew everything about every player," MacKenzie said. "And he knew that I had gone undefeated against Harvard at Yale. He wasn't just saying that to say it."

MacKenzie was almost shocked by how much Stengel knew about his players. He recalled a bus trip into Manhattan from the airport, on which Stengel was holding forth about a player and "this guy from Vanderbilt."

"Casey had already gotten off the bus, when I realized the player he was talking about was me," MacKenzie said: the "guy from Vanderbilt" was MacKenzie's coach in the minor leagues.

He Fit in Right Away

By the middle of the season, the players were starting to get in a rhythm with each other. No one demonstrated a better understanding of the Mets system than the new catcher, Joe Pignatano.

One day, Pignatano was warming up pitchers, and Casey Stengel called the bullpen.

"Get Nelson up," he instructed Pignatano.

Pignatano looked around at the Mets relievers, none with a first or last name of anything even close to Nelson. So he did the only thing he could think of: he slapped a baseball down on the pitching slab and yelled, "Nelson!"

The right-handed Bob Miller, who was mysteriously known to Stengel as Nelson, began warming up. (Equally mysterious, but seemingly related, Stengel referred to broadcaster Lindsey Nelson as Lindsey Miller.)

In the same game, two innings later, Casey Stengel called Pignatano back and asked him to "get Blanchard up."

Pignatano replied, "Blanchard? What do I do, take a cab across the river or walk?"

Pignatano assumed Stengel was thinking of Johnny Blanchard, whom he had coached on the Yankees. Although Stengel might have run into some confusion had he made the same request at Yankee Stadium: Johnny Blanchard was primarily a catcher, not a pitcher.

After the game, Stengel confronted Pignatano about the confusion in the bullpen. Pignatano defended himself.

"Don't get mad at me," Pignatano told Stengel, according to the *Sunday News*. "You're the one. I don't know who your players are. How am I supposed to know that Bobby Miller is Bobby Nelson?"

Communication with the Pitchers

Casey Stengel must have had sympathy for his pitchers. He was frequently out on the mound to offer encouraging words. For example, Ken MacKenzie was pitching once, and he watched unhappily as the infield made four errors in a row. When Stengel came out to the mound, MacKenzie's first thought was, "What did I do?" All Stengel said was, "You know they can't make the double play."

In another instance, Ray Daviault was on the mound when the Mets' opponents managed to load the bases without hitting a ball out of the infield. Stengel had these words for Daviault: "You'd better strike somebody out. They can't fumble that."

Sometimes Stengel's instructions were even less specific. Craig Anderson recalled coming in as a reliever early in the season. Stengel told him, "You know what to do."

"It was a bunt situation," said Anderson. "I think the next guy bunted the ball and I went over to field it, and I turned around and my first baseman, (Jim) Marshall, was standing right behind me. So that didn't do any good.

"I read in the paper the next day that I didn't do what he wanted. But he didn't tell me what he wanted. That was the way he communicated. You'd read it in the papers the next day. 'I wanted Anderson to push this guy back so we could see if he was going to bunt …' He didn't say that. If he really wanted to say something to us, he didn't call us into his office. He'd call the press."

The Man Behind the Curtain

On a regular baseball team, the manager calls the bullpen with a well-defined idea about what or who he needs.

"Managers usually have a real strict way of calling the bullpen, real quick, get this guy up, or in the minor leagues, you use a hand signal," Craig Anderson said. "As a reliever with the Mets, I'd be in the bullpen warming up and warming up, and I never knew if they were going to put me in the game. Other managers I could usually tell when they were going to put me in the game. But I could never tell. I remember one day I threw so much my arm was just hanging. I was glad they didn't put me in that day."

The man behind the Mets' pitching curtain was coach Red Ruffing, who made more of the decisions than fans suspected. Casey Stengel regularly opened his call to pitching coach Red Ruffing like this:

"Who've you got down there?"

Dutifully, Ruffing would oblige Stengel and list all the relievers.

Stengel would listen carefully, then say something perhaps as specific as, "Get me a right hander."

"If Ruffing liked you, he got you up," Craig Anderson said. "I guess he liked me, because he got me up 50 times."

That explained the mystery for Ken MacKenzie. "I never understood why Anderson pitched so much more than I did," he said.

A Shutout Is a Sure Way to Win

On July 27, Al Jackson logged his third shutout of the season, with a 1-0 win at St. Louis that ended the Mets' losing streak at 11. Not only did the Mets play defense well enough to support Jackson, but they scored in the third inning in a way that generally befit their opponents: without hitting a ball out of the infield. Catcher Choo Choo Coleman hit an infield single to third base, then went to second on Jackson's sacrifice bunt. Richie Ashburn struck out for the second time that day, but Rod Kanehl followed with a grounder to second, and Coleman scored on second baseman Julio Gotay's error.

New York held a lead through the eighth inning of the second game, then lost it when the Cardinals' Charlie Jarvis hit a three-run homer. The 11-game losing streak had not topped June's 17-game slide, and when it was over, the Mets' record was 25-74, and the team was 41-1/2 games out of first place.

Choo Choo

Mets catcher Choo Choo Coleman remained a charming puzzle throughout the season. He spoke very rarely, which Sherman (Roadblock) Jones thought was the result of a speech impediment. The result was an almost totally mysterious catcher.

"He could speak English, but he only spoke one-two-word sentences," said Craig Anderson. "It worried our pitchers a little bit, because there is a communication factor with pitchers and catchers. It took me a little while to get used to him, because he didn't say much, and I was never really sure what he was thinking behind the plate."

Apparently, Coleman was also unsure what he was thinking behind the plate. He occasionally forgot what sign he'd put down. He would put down the sign for "one," then move into position for "two." Sometimes he had to remind himself what he'd done.

"When he gave a sign, Choo Choo would get down in a crouch and he'd put his head down between his legs, and he'd watch himself put the one down," Anderson said. "He'd look at his fingers every time he gave a sign. And he'd look up and me and I would nod my head yes, and then he would nod his head yes. And then I would pitch. And the next time, he'd put a two down, and he'd look up at me, and I'd shake my head no, and he'd shake his head no and change the sign."

Clarence Coleman
BRACE PHOTO

Experience Doesn't Mean Everything

Early August brought the following exchange between Casey Stengel and Choo Choo Coleman, his speedy catcher, according to the *New York Times*.

"You ain't in Syracuse any more," Stengel said, explaining the importance of communication between the pitcher and catcher on plays at first base. "Thousands of people are here. You got to yell to the pitcher, 'Cover first.' You got to scream."

Coleman, who had spent the first part of the season in the minor leagues, couldn't see the logic of it.

"I figure they should know what to do up here," he said.

Happy Birthday, Old Perfessor

The Mets celebrated Casey Stengel's 72nd birthday in St. Louis on July 29, between games in a doubleheader. Stengel's actual date of birth was July 30, which was an open date for the players, so George Weiss flew to Missouri and the team ate birthday cake with its manager there.

Without regard for the occasion, the Mets lost both games that day. The first was by far the more frustrating of the two, as the score was tied with the bases loaded and two out in the Cardinals' half of the eighth inning. Ken Boyer hit a broken-bat single that scored two runs and moved Stan Musial to third base. Boyer then tried to steal second base and got caught in a rundown between Charlie Neal, who was playing shortstop, and Marv Throneberry.

Neal threw the ball to Throneberry, who chased Boyer all the way back to second base. Amidst the confusion, Musial scored from third, laughing all the way to home plate.

The Mets scored two more runs in the top of the ninth inning, making Musial's run the winner in the Mets' 6-5 loss.

Frank Thomas's Hot Streak

At the beginning of August, Frank Thomas hit two home runs in three consecutive games. The Mets lost all three.

Thomas opened his hot streak in the Polo Grounds, in a twilight game against Philadelphia's Jack Hamilton. He had hit 20 home runs already that season, so nothing was said after he hit the first one. His second was a grand slam.

"I had these glasses on that were yellow glasses and made the field look like it was daylight," Thomas said. "I'm rounding the bases, and as I come into the dugout, Casey said, 'Where'd you get those glasses?'

"I said 'I got them from the trainer, Gus Mauch.'

"And he said, 'Tell them to order a gross of them for the other players.'"

Stoked by Thomas's six RBI, the Mets stayed even with the Phillies for eight innings, then had the tying runs in scoring position with one out in the ninth inning. Jim Hickman and Joe Pignatano struck out to end the 11-9 game in Philadelphia's favor.

The next day, Art Mahaffey took the mound for the Phillies, and Thomas hit two more, as did Marv

Throneberry. All came with no one on, whereas Mahaffey managed a grand slam in the third inning, and Philadelphia won 9-4.

The Phillies were off August 3, having improved their record by two games, courtesy of the Mets, and Cincinnati pulled into the Polo Grounds. The Mets cut the Reds' lead to a run with a seventh-inning rally in which Thomas hit his second home run of the game and Marv Throneberry and Choo Choo Coleman hit the right field stands. Cincinnati responded by extending its lead to the final score of 8-6.

They Could Swing the Bats

The Mets weren't short on home runs. In fact, as a team, the Mets hit 139 home runs in 1962, only one less than the second-place Dodgers. The problem was, so many of them were solo shots—nine in a row in early August. Frank Thomas, who hit fourth, managed quite a number of these and, reportedly, frustrated Casey Stengel with his inability or refusal to play small ball. To be fair, Thomas was strictly a pull hitter, which meant that sometimes he hit Polo Grounds home runs without even trying.

Stengel, as always, had a unique way of expressing himself on these matters. For example, promotional signs down the foul lines offered a boat to the Met who hit the sign the most.

"If you hit the sign on the fly they would give you five points and on the bounce, they'd give you three, and if you hit it on the ground they'd give you one," Thomas explained. "The points would be added up at the end of the season, and whoever had the most points would get the boat. I was up at the plate one time, and I was strictly a pull hitter, and I hit one foul. I heard Casey in the stands, 'If you want to be a sailor, join the Navy.'"

Losing to the Mets

The Cincinnati Reds arrived in New York with their eyes on one thing, and it wasn't the Mets. Heading into their early-August five-game series in the Polo Grounds, the defending pennant winners were 8-1/2 games out of first place, behind the Dodgers and the Giants. The Reds had won each of their first eight games with the Mets; there was no reason to think they couldn't significantly improve their position in the standings after five games in New York, and manager Fred Hutchinson told the sportswriters exactly that.

"If they're going to make a move toward the pennant, now's the time to do it," he said.

Winning the first game of the series only made Hutchinson more confident. To open the next day's double-header, he selected 34-year-old pitcher Johnny Klippstein, who had not been a regular starter since 1957, when he played for the Dodgers.

Klippstein didn't last an inning. The Mets inflated his ERA significantly, giving him six runs to think about before Hutchinson sent Ted Wills in to end the inning. The Mets beat up on Wills, too, and won the first game 9-1.

"We were all riled up," said Felix Mantilla. "We'd seen that article, where Fred Hutchinson, the manager, was saying we're going to sneak up on the Dodgers because they have to play the Giants, and they're going to beat up on each other, and then we'll sneak up on them because we have to play the Mets."

The Reds took New York a little more seriously in the second game, enough to play the game under protest when a slow rain dampened the game's start. But the skies cleared up and stayed that way until Frank Thomas hit his 26th home run of the season to win the game 3-2 in the 14th inning.

After the game, the Mets spied on Hutchinson, who demonstrated his legendary fiery temper in the visitors' dugout.

"We watched him through binoculars breaking all the lights in the dugout," Mantilla said. "He was breaking all kinds of things, smashing them up."

Hutchinson told his players he didn't want to see a single one of them in clubhouse, then sat alone in the dugout for a long time to make sure they were gone. After the game, he headed to Toots Shor's to take the edge off.

"When he got down there, who was sitting at the bar, but Casey Stengel, who bought him a couple drinks," said Jack Lang. "As Casey was leaving, he had a chauffeured car that the Mets provided him, and he said, 'Can I give you a ride?'

"And Hutchinson said, 'You already have.'"

Cincinnati split the next day's doubleheader with the Mets as well, and finished the series 10 games out of first place. The Mets stayed in the same place they'd started: 44 back.

Out with the Old, In with the New

On August 5, the Mets set a significant attendance mark when 15,402 fans paid to see a doubleheader with the Cincinnati Reds. The ticket sales brought the Mets' home attendance to 667,191, which meant that more people paid to see the Mets in the first two-thirds of their inaugural season than had paid to see the Giants in their full final season.

The Winning Double-Play Combo

The Mets went to the West Coast for the final time in the second week of August. This time they brought with them a new weapon: the double-play combination of Charlie Neal at shortstop, Rod Kanehl at second base, and—hold on to your hats—Marv Throneberry at first. The trio combined for three of the Mets' double plays in the 5-2 win over the Giants on August 8 and brought the team's total to 27 since Kanehl started playing second base on July 24.

"I had played a lot of second base in the minor leagues, and when Charlie Neal got hurt, Casey put me in at second," Kanehl said (Neal had surgery to remove a cyst on his hand). "I did quite well, and I think Mantilla played short. When Charlie Neal's hand healed, Casey put him in at short, and left me at second. There were a lot of ground balls, and we made a lot of double plays. The month of July we did gangbusters in 1962. I was hitting over .300, and having a lot of fun.

"We were playing good ball—we weren't winning, but we were playing good ball. Richie Ashburn was hitting good, and he would lead off, and I would hit second, and we had a lot of hit-and-runs."

Extra Base on Balls

Kanehl managed one of his favorite baseball memories at Candlestick Park, against pitcher Jack Sanford. He stole second base on a walk:

"I tried to bunt, and it went foul," Kanehl said. "I tried to bunt again, and it went foul up the line. And he said, you want on base that bad, I'll just drill you. He was mad. Well, he ended up walking me."

Sanford had his head down and was slamming the ball into his glove as Kanehl walked to first. Orlando Cepeda, the first baseman, had a habit of turning to the right field and raking the dirt smooth with his head down, and the second baseman Chuck Hiller and shortstop Jose Pagan were looking into the outfield.

"As I got to first base, I realized, nobody's looking," Kanehl said. "So I took off for second and went in standing up."

After the game, the Mets boarded their plane, and once the flight was in the air, the Mets broadcasters cornered Kanehl.

"We were standing around the galley, and they said, 'Rod, the next time you do something like that, let us know. We were broadcasting, and we said, Kanehl draws ball four, and they cut away for a commercial. We all got up to get a soft drink or a cup of coffee or something, and we come back and you're on second base and we don't know how you got there. And we can't explain it to the broadcast audience.'

"They said, 'The next time you do something like that, try to give us some advance notice.'"

No Pennant?

By August 10, the pennant was officially, mathematically out of the Mets' reach. After 114 games, they had won 30 and lost 84. On the same day, the first-place Dodgers improved their record to 79-38, which meant that even if, by some divine intervention, the Mets won 48 straight to end the season, they still couldn't have caught up with the Dodgers.

In what passed for more encouraging news, they were only 10 games out of ninth place.

Al Jackson's Very Long Night

Al Jackson lost 20 games before the 1962 season ended. None of them took longer than the Mets 3-1 loss to Philadelphia on August 14.

Jackson had pitched plenty of complete games, and it looked like he would get the win when the Mets loaded the bases in the top of the ninth with only one out. Well, Gene Woodling hit into a double play. Jackson retired the next three Phillies, and as he'd only given up two hits, both of them singles and none since the fifth inning, the coaching staff had no qualms about leaving him to pitch a few extra innings.

Jackson pitched brilliantly, retiring every Philadelphia batter he faced through the 11th inning. He watched from the dugout as the Mets failed to score Choo Choo Coleman from second in the tenth inning, then left Joe Christopher (running for Frank Thomas) on second in the 11th.

"They tried to take me out after the 11th inning, but I said, 'No, I'm all right,'" Jackson said. He was certain the game was almost over.

It almost was. Ashburn walked, then stole second in the 12th, but the Mets left him there, too. Finally, in the 13th inning, Charlie Neal hit a triple with no outs. Jackson allowed himself to feel a little excitement as the Mets loaded the bases.

"He was supposed to go home, we were going to win the game," Jackson recalled.

Then Joe Pignatano grounded directly into a double play.

"We got out of the inning without a run," Jackson said. "Oh, now I got to pick myself up and go out there again. I knew I was tired, and I did it to myself, because I thought we were going to win right there."

Jackson pitched two more scoreless innings. He might have pitched a third, but Marv Throneberry missed Tony Gonzalez's grounder to first and Gonzalez went to second base. Bob Oldis hit a single to right—the first hit Jackson had allowed since the 12th inning—and Gonzalez went to third base. Jackson walked the next batter, and Mel Roach hit a two-run single to end the game.

Jackson had thrown 215 pitches in the 15-inning game, which lasted four hours and 35 minutes.

Forty years later, Jackson found himself telling the story to some of the current Met pitchers.

"I told them, I pitched complete games, and extra-inning games," Jackson said. "And I think (Mets lefty) Al Leiter said, 'Didn't they have any other pitchers?'"

I Spy ... on Felix Mantilla

Felix Mantilla was in a slump, and Casey Stengel called the sometimes-shortstop into his office and confronted him with a batting average that had dropped from more than .300 to less than .280.

"Maybe it's the pitchers who are getting me out," Mantilla suggested.

No, Stengel responded, it was Mantilla's work ethic. He was, the manager suggested, spending too much time out on the town, not getting enough sleep, and coming to the ballpark tired. The club was assigning a private detective to tail Mantilla and get to the bottom of the problem.

(Though Stengel told Mantilla the Mets had hired someone to follow him, the idea almost certainly belonged to George Weiss. He always believed that hitting slumps were the result of decadent behavior. Stengel probably thought he was doing Mantilla a favor—if the infielder had been keeping late hours or illicit company, he could stop before he got caught.)

Mantilla insisted he had not been doing anything wrong. One night after a ball game, he was walking down the street, and he saw the detective following him.

"I walked up to him and I said, 'I know who you are. And you can go back to Casey Stengel or George Weiss or whoever sent you, and you tell them to buy you a new pair of shoes, because you're going to wear those out,'" Mantilla recalled.

"And he said, 'I don't know you.' But I said, 'I know who you are.' And I guess he did go back to Casey because that was the last I saw of him."

Mantilla said he'd heard the club had assigned a detective to Jim Hickman, too, though Hickman never knew about it.

Occasionally the fans followed Mantilla as well, often from the ballpark all the way back to his Manhattan apartment.

"I felt it was a little strange," Mantilla said. "Because we weren't that good of a ball club."

The Debut of the Fan Club

The Marvelous Marv Throneberry fan club made its debut at the Polo Grounds on August 18, as the Mets lost both games in a doubleheader with St. Louis. The enthusiastic youths wore T-shirts emblazoned with large letters, so if they stood in the right order, they spelled MARV! (except the exclamation point was upside down.)

Occasionally they reversed themselves to spell "VRAM!"

They waved a banner on which they had printed, "Cranberry, Strawberry, We Love Throneberry."

And they danced on the dugout and were promptly ejected. They bought another round of tickets and came back in to watch the end of game, for which their hero rewarded them with a home run.

"Twenty-five years after he was gone, you would still see in the crowd—V-R-A-M—which was Marv spelled backwards," said Dixie Throneberry, Marv's widow. "And in the crowd they would say, 'Cranberry, Strawberry, we still want Throneberry.'"

Choo Choo on the Air

Choo Choo Coleman had hit the first, albeit unofficial, Met home run in an exhibition game, and only grew more popular with the fans, but his notable reticence made it hard for the broadcasters to pull him into the spotlight. In some ways, they didn't want him there: they were afraid he wouldn't say anything.

Finally Ralph Kiner bowed to public pressure and invited Coleman onto his post-game show. He related the following story, which he swears is 100 percent true.

Kiner started with an easy question: "How did you get your nickname?"

Coleman answered, "I don't know."

Kiner knew Coleman might be difficult, but he hadn't counted on that. He panicked. He asked the first question that popped into his mind.

"What's your wife's name, and what's she like?"

Coleman answered: "Her name is Mrs. Coleman, and she likes me."

Kiner had invited Roger Craig to be on the show with Coleman, and after that exchange, Craig ended up doing most of the talking.

Welcome Back, Gil Hodges

Gil Hodges put on his Mets uniform August 20 for the first time in more than a month. Eleven pounds lighter and still getting back into shape, the first baseman participated in running and throwing drills. Batting practice was still a few days away, but Hodges was hoping to come back to play the last two weeks of the season.

He sat on the bench and watched as Pittsburgh swept the Mets, 2-0 and 6-3, in a doubleheader. The Mets had now lost 12 in a row. The right-handed Bob Miller started the second game, but after the Bucs took a two-run lead in the fourth inning on a single, a double, a walk and a wild pitch, Miller was gone. It was his 10th loss of the season and the 32nd time since 1959 that he'd failed to complete a game.

Gil Hodges
BRACE PHOTO

Throneberry Saves the Day

Roger Craig, pitching in relief, took the loss in the first game of a doubleheader with the Pirates on August 21. The Mets had a two-run lead when he entered the game; Felix Mantilla took care of that with a wild throw that ushered three Pirates across home plate in the ninth inning. It was the Mets' 13th loss in a row and Craig's 20th of the season, which made him the first pitcher to lose so many since the Cubs' Glen Hobbie lost 20 in 1960, and everyone felt bad about that.

"Roger Craig was our number-one pitcher, and he should have been our number-one reliever," said Rod Kanehl. "While it was going on, he wasn't disgruntled. He knew he had this position on the team, and it was his job to go out and pitch every fourth or fifth day. He knows we tried. He just couldn't pitch more than five or six innings, and we had no relief. We didn't have anyone who could pitch more than five or six innings."

Marvelous Marv Throneberry couldn't do anything to help Craig in the first game, but he did single-handedly end the Mets' losing streak in the second game of the double-header.

Ironically, Throneberry wasn't even in the lineup, as the left-handed Harvey Haddix started the game for Pittsburgh. Throneberry, a left-handed batter, watched most of the game from the dugout, until he finally broke into the coaching lineup. After Solly Hemus, who was coaching third base, was ejected for arguing, Casey Stengel began platooning his coaches. First Stengel took over at third base. Then he moved

Cookie Lavagetto to third base and sent Richie Ashburn to coach first base.

When the right-handed Elroy Face relieved Haddix with a 4-1 lead in the ninth, Stengel sent Ashburn to pinch-hit (single to right) and Throneberry wound up coaching first base. Felix Mantilla singled home Joe Christopher (Haddix had walked him to open the inning), and now, with two men on, Stengel signaled Throneberry to the plate.

Throneberry nailed a three-run homer to the right upper deck.

Mrs. Payson was sitting in the stands, right next to Dixie Throneberry.

"She said, 'Isn't he marvelous?'" Throneberry's widow recalled.

Good Guy Throneberry

At the end of 1962, the New York sportswriters presented Marv Throneberry with the Epstein "Good Guy award," and Dixie Throneberry said she thought the writers had their own reasons for doing so.

"I think that was because most of the sportswriters knew that they had stretched the truth quite a bit," said Throneberry's widow. "And they decided to give him that award because he was a good guy about it. There's so much myth mixed in with so much legend mixed in with the truth, I don't think he got the appreciation that he should have gotten."

When the writers gave him the award, Dick Young included the story of Throneberry's ninth-inning heroics against Pittsburgh in the program. He included the following exchange between Richie Ashburn and Throneberry in the clubhouse.

"Hey Marvelous," Ashburn said. "Do you realize that if you keep going like this, you'll lose all your fans?"

"Don't worry," Throneberry replied. "I can get them all back in one lousy night."

He didn't have to wait too long. The San Francisco Giants were in town the next night, August 22. Throneberry scored two runners when Jose Pagan dropped his pop-up, then got thrown out trying to stretch his hit into a triple.

Easy Money

Frank Thomas grew up without any money for a glove, and when he reached the major leagues, he liked to say he could catch anybody's fastball barehanded.

"When I was a little kid I was very poor," Thomas said. "I thought that was the way life was supposed to be. So they couldn't afford a glove for me, so I played fast pitch softball —I played shortstop—and I got my hands accustomed to that. When you know what you're doing, you won't have any problems. You give a little bit with the throw."

As a professional ballplayer, Thomas occasionally made a little money off the trick. When San Francisco came to town, Richie Ashburn bet Willie Mays $100 that Thomas could catch Mays's best fastball without a glove.

"We were warming up below the stands," Thomas said. "Mays came down his side, and Richie says, 'Want to make a quick hundred?'

"Willie said, 'Yes I do.'

"Richie said, 'I bet you Thomas can catch your fastball barehanded.'

"Willie said, 'No, no he can't.' So we went down by the dugout and drew a line 60 feet, 6 inches, and I thought Willie said he was ready so I dropped my glove and I caught it. Then he went back to Richie and said, 'I'm not warm yet, but let's make that a 10 dollar bet.'

"He never paid me. Every time I see him, maybe at the bat dinner or when they have these old-timers' games, I say, 'Hey Willie, when are you going to pay me?'

"He says, 'Look at all the publicity you got out of it.'"

The Dodgers Are Back

The Dodgers came to town just in time for Gil Hodges night. It was Hodges's second honorary event—he'd been similarly celebrated in 1957, on Gil Hodges day at Ebbets Field. After Hodges received all manner of gifts, from a complete home workbench to a case of champagne to a shotgun (courtesy of Duke Snider and Hodges's former teammates), the Mets honored their teammate with a 6-3 win.

Thinking about that final three-game series with the Dodgers reminded Craig Anderson of the following story:

"Choo Choo Coleman was very quick behind the plate, with a ball in the dirt, he moved real well, and he had a very quick throwing arm and a very quick release. One night, we're playing the Dodgers, and Willie Davis is batting. Willie Davis was known for losing the bat, it would come out of his hands. And this time, there was a runner on first base, Richie Ashburn was in right field.

"Davis swung and missed a pitch and his bat came around and flew out of his hands, and it hit Edna Stengel. She was sitting right by the dugout. I don't think it injured her seriously, but she was 70 years old, so of course, this bat was flying, and when it hit her, a convergence of security and trainers rushed over to Edna.

"Well, in the meantime, Choo Choo decided to try to pick the runner off first base. So he jumps, and fires one at first base. Well the first baseman was watching the bat go in the stands, and the runner was watching the bat go in the stands, and the Dodger coach, almost everybody was watching the bat and Edna, and the ball sailed way out there in right field.

"No one was moving, because Choo Choo had just fired that thing down there and nobody saw him do it. It took a while before somebody realized there was a live ball in right field, and then there was a panic. Ashburn finally looked around for the ball, and they were hollering from the bullpen. It was right behind him."

Sheer Helplessness

By the time Craig Anderson took the mound against the Dodgers on August 26, the Mets weren't just out of first place. They were mathematically out of seventh place, and unofficially out of eighth and ninth too.

By the time Anderson left the mound, he was unofficially out of his mind.

He pitched the first 5-1/3 innings and watched helplessly as the infield made enough errors to give the Dodgers eight unearned runs. Of course, Anderson also allowed eight hits and walked four. The damage was staggering. When Bob Moorhead came in to close the sixth inning, he inherited an 11-0 ballgame.

"I might have given up a single here or there, but then there'd be like two errors," Anderson said. "It was unbelievable. I think that I was in that game five-plus innings, and I'm still pitching. That would never happen today. They probably sympathized with me, but they probably should have taken me out anyway. I was a sinkerball pitcher, and I gave up a lot of ground balls, so I needed good infield support. When I didn't get it, it was a disaster. I probably walked a couple guys, but then I'd get a double-play ball and they'd boot it. That game, I still remember that game. I knew I was pitching well enough to stay in there, and Stengel could have taken me out, but he left me in."

It was Anderson's 13th consecutive loss, making him the first major league pitcher to lose 13 in a row since 1948, when the Cubs' Bob McCall suffered the same fate.

No. 100

On August 29, Jay Hook pitched 10 innings as the Mets lost their 100th game of the year, 3-2, to host Philadelphia. It was the first time since 1912 that a New York team had lost 100 games in a season.

"I hated to lose, but I really reached a point, for my own mental or emotional stability, I thought, I've got to cope with this somehow," Hook said. "And I'm sure that everybody kind of looked at it that way. I thought, 'If I take these all as seriously as I'm taking them, I'm going to be a basket case by the end of the season.' That was the wrong attitude. I shouldn't even have been thinking that way."

Self-Sabotage

Failure finally got to Bob Moorhead. He went in to relieve in three straight games at the end of August and never stayed in for more than an inning. After pitching the bottom of the eighth inning in St. Louis—and giving the Cardinals their last run in their 10-5 win on September 1—Moorhead was so frustrated, he punched the dugout door.

He fractured two knuckles on his pitching hand and missed the rest of the season.

Ashburn's Temporary Amnesia

On September 3, Richie Ashburn had the kind of game that every Met deserved, which is to say he couldn't remember a thing about it.

In the fifth inning of the first game of a doubleheader at Pittsburgh, Ashburn ran after a foul ball, crashed into the wall of the Mets' bullpen, and fell face first to the ground. After a brief rest and an argument that the ball was foul, the hit was ruled a ground-rule double and Ashburn returned to his place in the outfield. When Dick Groat hit a line drive his way, Ashburn turned the wrong way. In his final chance at bat, Ashburn struck out chasing a low and inside pitch.

After the game, which the Mets lost 2-0, Ashburn complained that ball had been foul and admitted he felt a little dizzy still. A reporter commented that it was a tough loss.

"You mean we lost the game?" Ashburn said, according to the *Times*. "We didn't win this game? What was the score? How did we lose it? We didn't lose it."

At that point, Joe Pignatano called Gus Mauch, the trainer.

"I swear, Gus, I can't remember a thing about the game," Ashburn said. "We didn't lose, did we?"

Mauch and Joseph Feingold, the Pirates' team doctor, agreed that Ashburn should go to the hospital. Ashburn protested.

"I'm good enough to play," he told Mauch. "I can play in the second one. I just can't remember, that's all."

He was back the next night, pinch-hit a single in the Mets' 5-1 loss, and joked, "The way we've been going, maybe it's too bad I didn't forget the whole year."

Gus Mauch
DONALD UHRBROCK/TIME LIFE PICTURES/GETTY IMAGES

The More Mets, the Merrier

In early September, the Mets brought young talent onto the team. Ed Kranepool, the bonus baby, came up from Class D ball. The team claimed Galen Cisco and Larry Foss on waivers. Foss remembered joining the team in Houston.

"I walked into the clubhouse in Houston," he said. "And Stengel told me this was for the ballplayers only. He didn't know who I was, or that I'd been traded or what."

An Unusual Tie

Shortly after 7 p.m. on September 9, the Mets' last game of an early September three-game series at Houston ended with the score tied at 7-7. Temperatures between 90 and 100 degrees had postponed the game from its 2:30 start to a hopefully cooler 4:30 start, then two short downpours further delayed the game. Felix Mantilla figured in both the sixth- and seventh-inning runs that tied the game for the Mets.

The game was scheduled to resume where it stopped when the Colt .45s traveled to the Polo Grounds at the end of September, but rain falls in New York, too. The tie was abandoned and another game with the Colts was cancelled entirely. As a result, the Mets' accurate final record for the 1962 season was 40-120-1.

Records Falling Like Rain

The Mets broke a number of major league records in 1962. The first one to fall was the number of home runs allowed by a team. The Mets set the National League record on September 14, when the Reds' Vada Pinson hit a home run, No. 186 against the Mets. New York won the game, and also bested the record previously held by St. Louis. The next day, the Mets lost to the Reds, gave up home run No. 187, and tied the record set by the Kansas City Athletics in 1956.

By September 18, the Mets had the record all to themselves. The same day the Colts' Merritt Ranew hit home run No. 188 against New York in the fourth inning of the second game of a doubleheader, Casey Stengel celebrated his 50th year in baseball. For the achievement, Stengel received a gold key to City Hall, a cocktail shaker from the National League, a silver bowl from the Mets, and a tape recorder from the New York baseball writers. For their less distinguished watermark, the Mets didn't get anything.

Luck, Good and Bad

The Mets didn't have a monopoly on bad luck in the Polo Grounds, as Houston's Bob Aspromonte discovered during a September 20 doubleheader. He had set the National League record with 57 error-free games at third base, which abruptly came to an end when he kicked an Elio Chacon grounder in the eighth inning of the opener.

The night an error-free player made a mistake, an error-prone player won a prize. Marv Throneberry was awarded a boat worth $7,000 for hitting the Howard Clothes sign in right field more than any other Met. Richie Ashburn won a $5,000 boat for being the most valuable Met.

Six days later, the team's legal advisor explained that because Throneberry earned his boat in a contest of skill, he would have to pay income tax on it. Ashburn's, which was a gift, was not taxable. Throneberry, it turned out, lived about 300 miles from a body of water, though perhaps it was for the best. When Ashburn put his boat in the water off the coast of New Jersey, it sank. According to Ralph Kiner, no one had installed the drainage plug.

Two 20-Game Losers and Other Historical Footnotes

Al Jackson pitched 2-1/3 innings in a September 22 game with the Cubs, just long enough to give up five runs on seven hits and absorb his 20th loss of the season. For the first time since 1936, a National League team had two 20-game losers. (The Phillies' Bucky Walters and Joe Bowman both lost 20 in 1936).

That loss was No. 116 for the Mets, and as they pulled within a game of the major league mark, they seemed to sense they were making history. In the same game, the youngest Met, 17-year-old Ed Kranepool, relieved the oldest Met, 38-year-old Gil Hodges. Richie Ashburn played the ninth inning at second base, the first time in his 14 major league seasons that he played anywhere other than the outfield.

Rod Kanehl had played every position except pitcher and catcher during the 1962 season, and late in the season the club's management gave him the opportunity to play all nine.

"You know, there have been several players who've played every position in a nine-inning game," Kanehl said. "I turned them down. I mean, we were bad ballplayers, but we weren't clowns."

The Last Win at Home

On September 23, the Mets hosted the Chicago Cubs for their last home game of the season. Frank Thomas hit his 33rd home run in the sixth inning to tie the score 1-1 and, three innings later, Thomas hit a single to score Choo Choo Coleman with the winning run.

More than 10,000 fans came to watch what they thought was the Mets' last game in the Polo Grounds. The new stadium in Flushing Meadows was scheduled to be ready for the beginning of the 1963 season, which signaled a death knell for the Polo Grounds. Throughout the Mets' last game there in 1962, the public address announcer played several sentimental songs for the old ballpark, and when Casey Stengel finished his on-field television interview, the fans watched him jog 475 feet to the clubhouse, as "Auld Lang Syne" filled the stadium.

Bob Miller's Happy Ending

The right-handed Bob Miller struggled valiantly against his own so-called negative statistic through September. On September 10, he lost his 12th game of the season, and if he lost another, he would become the first pitcher in major league baseball to lose 13 without winning one. He pitched a two-hitter through eight innings in the Mets' last home game, but Roger Craig pitched the ninth, the Mets won it in the bottom of the last inning, and the win went to Craig.

On the next-to-last day of the season, Miller found redemption. Marv Throneberry scored Jim Hickman with a two-out double in the seventh inning to give New York a 2-1 lead—which Miller held through the ninth inning. It was his first complete game since September 3, 1959, and no doubt the first time a pitcher happily finished a season 1-12.

The Very End

The Mets ended their season on the road in Chicago.

"I'll never forget that, because the last pitch I ever threw in '62 was against Chicago in late September with the Cubs," said Larry Foss. "I remember Stengel saying, 'Who wants to throw? Who wants to pitch?' I raised my hand. I said, 'Hell yeah, let me get some more experience in here.'"

Those late-season pitches were Foss's last in the major leagues. Similarly, Joe Pignatano ended his major league career by hitting into a triple play, which finished the Mets' last game, a 5-1 loss to the Cubs.

After the season, most of the players went home from Chicago. Quite a few of them were glad the debacle was over. They had lost 120 games, bypassing the 1916 Philadelphia Athletics' mark of 117 losses.

Casey Stengel, who said he was shocked and sad about how the season had gone, tried to cheer his players up.

"Fellers, don't feel bad about this," he told them. "No one or two players could have done all this."

Only Frank Thomas was sad to see the season end. He had hit 34 home runs, only one short of the career-high 35 he hit in 1958.

"Why would you want something to end that you're doing well in?" Thomas said. "But it was a long season. What's great about the game of baseball, you can lose 15-0, but you start fresh again tomorrow."

Still Losing

In a cruel twist, the Mets managed to get worse even after they'd stopped playing. After their last game of the season, they were 60 games out of first place. The October play-off between the Dodgers and the Giants pushed them another half-game back before the World Series.

Casey Stengel had signed on for another year with the Mets, and he promised the team would be more successful.

"We'll do better in 1963," Stengel said. "For one thing, we'll know more about each other. This year, everything was new, including the manager and the coaches. We'll do better, all right, just wait and see."

From Worst to First

The front office did its best to revamp the Mets for 1963. When the team arrived for its home opener—still at the Polo Grounds, as the new stadium in Queens wasn't open yet—Frank Thomas was the only Original Met in his original position: left field. Charlie Neal played at third base, Ed Kranepool stood on first base, and Roger Craig pitched. Other '62 Mets were still hanging around, making their way into the lineup cards: Rod Kanehl, Craig Anderson, Choo Choo Coleman, Marv Throneberry, Cliff Cook.

Casey Stengel could see, from opening day, that the two-year-old Mets were going to have the same problems the inaugural Mets had, and they did. The Mets finished 51-111 that year, dead last.

The Mets moved to their new stadium the next year, named for Bill Shea, the man who had brought National League baseball back to New York. It didn't help. The Mets lost more than 100 games and finished in last place every year until 1966, when they lost 95 and finished a dizzying ninth. They dropped back into last place in 1967. Gil Hodges took over as manager the next year and led the club to ninth, one grateful game ahead of old enemy Houston. It made 1969 all the more incredible.

Forty-one games into the season, the Mets were on pace to finish as well as they had in 1968. They were 9 games behind the first-place Cubs, but they didn't take losing with quite the same levity as the original Mets.

"I'm tired of the old jokes about the Mets," pitcher Tom Seaver told Ralph Kiner. "Let Rod Kanehl and

Marvelous Marv laugh about the old Mets. We're out here to win. You know when we'll have champagne? When we win the pennant."

And they did. The Mets surged ahead, winning 82 of the next 121 to finish first in the National League East.

"They played the Cardinals and they beat them, and all they had to do was to win one more game and they'd won the division," recalled Craig Anderson. "I was at that game, I called and I got tickets. Of course that was a massive celebration. I went into the locker room. And then they said, come on up to the party, and the champagne was flowing."

The Mets swept the Braves, who had by then moved to Atlanta, to win the pennant. Then they beat the Orioles, four games to one, to win their first World Championship.

Seven years earlier, the Mets couldn't have swept the floor with a broom. And now they had won the World Series.

The championship was a true boon for the team and every fan it had ever had. If there was a drawback, it was a tiny one, and only a real nitpicker would bring it up: the innocence was gone. Never again would 100 losses bring laughter and joy to Mets fans. Now they wanted major leaguers.

Tale of the Tigers

More than 40 years later, every one of the 1962 Mets receives a handful of autograph requests in the mail each month. The seekers are either Mets fans fascinated by the inaugural team, or they are baseball junkies, interested in the team that still holds the record for the worst season of baseball's modern era.

The Mets nearly shrugged off that infamous label during the summer of 2003, when the Detroit Tigers amassed a record of 38-118 with six games left to play. They seemed certain to supplant the Mets, and in fact America's sportswriters had been drawing the comparison and keeping watch since the All-Star break.

By focusing on the Tigers, the nation also cast a backward glance at the 1962 Mets. None were proud custodians of the worst record in baseball, but none were eager to pawn it off on a new team, either.

"Alan Trammell, it was his first year of managing, and he's a good guy," Jay Hook said of Detroit's rookie manager. "He had a great playing record, he's been very loyal to Detroit, and I know how sportswriters are. If they broke that record, whenever they mentioned Trammell, there would be a tagline, and the tagline would be '… who managed the 2003 Tigers, who were the worst team in baseball.'"

The Tigers accomplished the improbable: they won five of their last six to finish a lousy, but not record-breaking or even record-tying, 43-119.

"They've got a bunch of young guys in Detroit," said Don Zimmer, who watched from the bench as the Yankees beat the Tigers five out of six times. "Two years from now, the Detroit Tigers might be a .500 ball club."

And the next time a team nears 120 losses, the phones of the 1962 Mets will still ring.

Chapter
1 0

WHERE ARE THEY NOW?

The Pitchers

CRAIG ANDERSON'S 16-game single-season losing streak remains one of the longer ones in major league history. He played in a handful of games over the next two years, losing his next three decisions, and his 19 consecutive losses remained a club record until Mets right-hander Anthony Young lost 27 straight between April 19, 1992, and July 28, 1993.

After baseball, he returned to Pennsylvania and went to work at Lehigh University, first in development, then in the athletic department and later as a baseball coach. He and his wife Judy recently retired to Dunnellon, Florida, where Anderson signed on as a part-time pitching coach at the local high school.

ROGER CRAIG returned to the Mets in 1963 and lost 20 more games, making him the first pitcher since 1906 to lose 20 games in two consecutive seasons. He played for the St. Louis Cardinals in 1964 and earned a win in the fourth game of the World Series with the Yankees, which the

Cardinals went on to win. He took his first major league managerial job with the Padres in 1978, then headed the Giants from the middle of 1985 to the end of 1992.

His 1962 performance is still a team record in three categories: losses (24), earned runs allowed (117), and hits allowed (261). (Jay Hook and Al Jackson both rank in the top 10 in those categories for their 1962 numbers too.)

On the occasion of Mets broadcaster Bob Murphy's retirement in 2003, Craig said of the 1962 season, "Everyone remembers I lost 20 games. What they don't remember is that I won 10, and the team only won 40."

LARRY FOSS went to spring training with the Mets in 1963 and never pitched a game, though he threw every day. One day the club was scheduled to play an exhibition game with West Point, and Foss was supposed to pitch.

"I said, 'You guys have been throwing me so much up here already, my arm is falling off, there's no way I can pitch.' Well, I mean, what are you going to do? If you do well, you're expected to, but if you don't, it's a lose-lose situation.

"I was traded the next week to Milwaukee, and Milwaukee sent me to Denver in the Pacific Coast League, triple-A ball, and I finished the season with Denver and hung 'em up."

Foss went on to work in oil and gas, then owned his own business in Steamboat Springs, Colorado, for a time. Now retired, Foss lives in Kansas and tries to golf every day, weather permitting.

"I'm in pretty good shape I guess," Foss said. "I guess it's better than the alternative."

JAY HOOK returned to the Mets in 1963, won four and lost 14. He played part of 1964 and called it quits. He had met his goal of five full seasons of major league baseball, in which he and his wife had moved more than 20 times.

"At the end of that time, I thought, I'm just an average player," Hook said. "If I was good enough to really excel, I would have stayed in longer. But I wasn't, and I decided, our oldest boy was starting school, and all this moving around was kind of a negative. At the end of five years, I thought I'd get into industry."

Hook began a long career in mechanical engineering and applied physics, then became a professor at Northwestern University, where he helped design an MBA program in manufacturing management.

WILLARD HUNTER pitched 63 innings for the Mets in 27 appearances in 1962, and compiled a 1-6 record and a 6.65 ERA. He popped back into the major leagues in 1964 and spent the season in relief for the Mets. That year was better for the team and for the lefty pitcher, who finished the season 3-3 with five saves.

After baseball, Hunter went on to work in computers. Now retired and living in Nebraska, he doesn't talk about the Mets. He put his brief stint as a major league baseball player behind him.

"He was famous at one time," his wife said, "And now he doesn't want to be noticed by anybody."

AL JACKSON lives in Port St. Lucie, Florida, the home of Mets spring training. He pitched three more years for the Mets, and though he never managed a winning record, he was the Mets' most consistently successful pitcher through

1965. He had his first winning season for St. Louis in 1967, then returned to the Mets for the 1968 season. He was traded to Cincinnati in the middle of June, 1969.

In 1999, he joined the Mets as a part-time coach and player development consultant.

From the Mets, **SHERMAN JONES** went on to Syracuse, where he pitched another month. Persistent shoulder pain sent him to a Raleigh doctor, who diagnosed him with acute gout, the result of excessive uric acid in his right shoulder joint. Jones rehabilitated his shoulder in the warm, mid-Atlantic weather, and rejoined Syracuse later in the season. His wife Amelia went into labor that summer, and he drove home from Knoxville to Kansas City to be with Amelia in time for the birth of their daughter, Sheila.

He pitched a little more that summer and made the International League all-star team, but Jones never pitched another game in the major leagues.

"I knew I had problems, my power had gone," Jones said. "I had a reasonable slider, but it wasn't powerful. A slider ain't worth a nickel if you don't have something to go with it."

Jones went to work for the Kansas City Police Department in 1965. He retired in 1988 and ran, successfully, for the Kansas House of Representatives, where he served two terms, then was elected to the Kansas Senate. He is now retired, and he and Amelia live in Kansas City, where the governor and everyone else still calls him Roadblock.

CLEM LABINE turned 36 in August of 1962. His few innings with the Mets marked the end of a 13-year career in the major leagues that included five trips to the World Series. He regretted, a little, allowing his career to end with such a sputter.

"All the rest of us, we were getting into our heyday, as far as being in ball clubs was concerned," said Labine, who lives in Florida now. "I should have said 'No' to Casey. I should have said, 'Thank you, but we have our careers.'"

KEN MACKENZIE went on to work and coach at his alma mater, Yale University. When Rod Kanehl's son Phil came to Yale, he sought out MacKenzie on the baseball diamond, though Kanehl didn't go out for the team.

MacKenzie lives in Connecticut and is at work on a book about the '62 season.

The right-handed ROBERT MILLER played for the Dodgers in 1963, and 11 years and six teams later returned to the Mets for the final season of his 17-year major league career. He died in a car accident in California in 1993, at age 54.

The first year of the Mets was the last of VINEGAR BEND MIZELL'S nine-year career in the major leagues. He did better in politics. He settled in North Carolina, where he was elected to the U.S. House of Representatives in 1968. After he lost his seat in 1974, he worked for both the Ford and Reagan administrations.

He died in February, 1999, at the age of 68, four months after he suffered a heart attack.

HERB MOFORD retired from baseball in 1963 and returned to Kentucky, where he settled into daily life as a tobacco farmer, "and that's what I've been doing ever since."

BOB MOORHEAD played two and a half more years of minor league baseball before he put on a Mets uniform again in 1965, and pitched his last major league game that September.

After baseball, he lived in Lemoyne, Pennsylvania, not far from his hometown of Chambersburg, and worked for, then retired from a trucking company. He died at home on December 3, 1986, at age 48.

The Catchers

HARRY CHITI played his last year of baseball in 1962. In his 10-year career in the majors, he played in 502 games, for seven different teams, and hit 41 home runs.

He and his wife, Catherine, and their two children, Dom and Cynthia, moved to Tennessee, where Chiti found a career in law enforcement, according to the *News Chief*, a Polk County, Florida, newspaper.

Dom grew into a talented left-handed pitcher, who was selected by the Atlanta Braves in the 1976 draft. Dom never played in the major leagues, but went on to become a valued advance scout. He worked with John Hart in Cleveland, then took on the title of "special assistant to the general manager" when he followed Hart to the Texas Rangers.

Harry and Catherine Chiti retired to Winter Haven, Florida, and Harry died January 31, 2002. Catherine still lives in Winter Haven, with their daughter Cynthia.

JOE GINSBERG played his last major league season with the 1962 Mets.

"It was sort of a fun year," he said. "It wasn't fun losing every day, but with all of us old pros, we did have a good time. Especially with thousands of people coming to the Polo Grounds every day."

He retired to Florida in 1986, travels to Detroit Tigers fantasy camps on occasion, and plays golf (15 handicap). For a while, he found himself doubly inscribed in the trivia books: once for being an original Met, once for playing both on the American League team with the best record—the 1954 Cleveland Indians won 111 games—and the National League team with the worst record. The Yankees broke the Indians' record with 114 wins in 1998, but none of the members of that team had also played for the 1962 Mets. (The 2001 Seattle Mariners own that record now. None of them were original Mets, either.)

The Infielders

GIL HODGES won three Gold Gloves and hit 370 home runs in 20 years as a player, and transitioned seamlessly into management. He returned to the Mets in 1968, taking the Mets from perennial losers to champions of the world in two seasons, a performance that earned Hodges the nickname "Miracle Worker." He continued to manage until April 2, 1972, when he died of a heart attack after playing a round of golf in Florida, where the Mets were in spring training. It was two days before his 48th birthday.

"When he died, that really was a crushing blow to baseball," Craig Anderson said. "I remember, I was on the bus with the Lehigh team and I was shocked when I heard. He was just a guy I was really happy to have met."

In spite of his successes as a player and manager, Hodges has not yet been inducted into the National Baseball Hall of Fame.

ROD KANEHL played two more years of baseball, both with the Mets. He returned to Wichita, Kansas, where he joined a semi-pro baseball team—the Dreamliners—and, with Charlie Neal as a teammate, won a national championship. His work for an insurance company relocated Kanehl, his wife and their four children to California, and when the insurance work dried up, the family stayed. Kanehl found work in restaurant management and recently took up caddying at a Palm Springs country club.

His own golf game is not so good.

"I played baseball so long, when I get a ball standing still on a tee, I'm going to take a good cut," he said. "I'm not going to get cheated."

The Mets traded **FELIX MANTILLA** to the Red Sox in December of 1962, and two seasons later, Mantilla hit a career-best 30 home runs. In 1966 he played his last season of major league baseball in Houston, and finished his 11-year career without letting his batting average dip below .215.

He managed a minor-league team in Canada, then moved to Milwaukee, where he'd started his baseball career with the Braves. He worked for a Milwaukee Boys and Girls Club until he retired. He and his wife have two children and four grandchildren, and every now and again they run into Mantilla's old teammate, fellow Wisconsinite John DeMerit.

JIM MARSHALL finished the 1962 season with the Pittsburgh Pirates and never played another major league baseball game.

"I felt I got a reprieve, to a certain extent," Marshall said. "So I didn't have to live through that entire year. Though it was the only time I hit .300 in my life."

He went on to a coaching career and managed the Chicago Cubs and the Oakland A's in the 1970s. The 1979 Oakland A's, under Marshall's stewardship, were only 12 wins better than the 1962 Mets. Suddenly, Marshall understood what Stengel had been going through, "and it was not a good feeling."

He has worked with the Arizona Diamondbacks since 1998, the team's first year. The team lost 97 games that year, won 100 the next year, and won the world series in 2001, record speed for an expansion team. Marshall is now the Diamondbacks' director of Pacific Rim scouting and lives in California.

MARV THRONEBERRY played 14 more games for the Mets in 1963 then called it quits. Rumor suggested that, when Mrs. Payson learned the Mets were sending Throneberry to the minors, the horseracing fan said, "I guess there's nothing to do but put him down." Payson set the record straight in 1968: "Send him down," she insisted.

Throneberry found a successful career in sales and public relations, and in the 1980s, jumped back into the spotlight as a pitchman for Miller Lite with the famous tagline, "I still don't know why they asked me to do this commercial."

He died in June 1994.

Five years later, Kansas City's George Brett was inducted into the National Baseball Hall of Fame, and took a tiny piece of Throneberry with him. Brett made most of his 3,154 hits with a Louisville Slugger T-85, a bat first designed for Marvelous.

"I wasn't there that long," **DON ZIMMER** said. "Blame three weeks on me, but don't blame the whole season on me."

Zimmer finished out the 1962 season with the Reds, and hit a respectable .250. He played two more years in the major leagues, first with Los Angeles, then with Washington, and finished his playing years in Japan. He managed in the minor leagues and coached for the Expos and the Padres before becoming the manager in San Diego in 1972. He went on to manage the Red Sox, the Rangers and the Cubs, where he was named the National League manager of the year in 1989, and joined Yankee manager Joe Torre's staff as a bench coach. Zimmer ran the team in 1999 when Torre was treated for prostate cancer. By the time Zimmer quit the Yankees after the 2003 season, he was 72, the same age as Casey Stengel at the end of 1962.

He and Richie Ashburn stayed friends forever, and Zimmer frequently drove from his home in St. Petersburg to Ashburn's winter home in Florida for games of Gin Rummy.

The Outfielders

RICHIE ASHBURN never played another day of major league baseball.

"He hit .306, and he retired at the end of the year, and I could never understand that," said Don Zimmer. "I guess it was two years later, I said to him, 'You hit .306, why'd you ever quit?'

"He said, 'I was afraid we were going to lose 120 games again the next year, and I didn't want to be a part of it.'"

Ashburn stepped seamlessly into the Philadelphia Phillies' broadcaster booth, where he worked for 35 years. He was elected to the National Baseball Hall of Fame in 1995, and died two years later of a heart attack in a Manhattan hotel. He was on the road with the Phillies.

GUS BELL appeared in six more major league games in 1963 and 1964. He died on May 7, 1995, at the age of 66, but his name lives on: One of his four sons, Buddy, went on to play 18 years in the major leagues, and Buddy's son David played his ninth major league season with the 2003 Phillies.

As recently as the summer of 2003, **JOE CHRISTOPHER** was making pre-Colombian paintings in his Baltimore home.

After he was cut by the Mets, **JOHN DEMERIT** went home to consider his options. Rather than take a pay cut and toil in the minor leagues, he went back to school, finished his master's degree, and got a job with a local insurance company. He found his way back to the green grass and baseball diamonds seven years later, when he became a director in the Parks and Recreation department in Port Washington, Wisconsin, where he worked for 26 years.

He is enjoying retirement, and continues to be mildly baffled by the attention he receives for having been an original Met.

"What about the 63 Mets or the 78 Mets, or whatever else?" DeMerit said. "I don't see the fascination there that some do. There's something in the New York scene that escapes me."

Perhaps the only original Met whose most successful years were truly in front of him, **JIM HICKMAN** played 12 more years of baseball. In 1963, he became the first Met to hit for the cycle, and stayed with the New York club through the 1966 season. After a year with the Dodgers, in which the outfielder actually pitched two innings (4.5 ERA, no decision) he settled in with the Cubs. In 1970, he hit .315 with 32 home runs, the *Sporting News* named him the National League comeback player of the year, and he scored the winning run in the 12th inning of the All-Star game.

After baseball, Hickman returned to Henning, Tennessee, population 802, where he farmed soybeans and tobacco for a dozen years. In 1985, the Cincinnati Reds hired him as a minor league hitting instructor, and Hickman worked his 17th season with the Reds minor leaguers in 2002. He wears No. 28 when he works with the Reds, but his heart is with the Mets.

"I'm still a Mets fan," Hickman said. "It's hard for me to forget my beginnings. The only time I probably wouldn't be a Mets fan is when they're playing Cincinnati."

BOBBY GENE SMITH, who proved inconsequential to the general state of the Mets' outfield, didn't stay in Chicago for too long either. In a little more than a month with the Cubs, he did only slightly better than he had with the Mets: two more hits in seven more at-bats. On June 5, 1962, the Cubs traded him to the St. Louis Cardinals, where he went on to hit .231 over the course of 91 games. It was his last full season in the major leagues; he played 23 games with the California Angels in 1965.

FRANK THOMAS still holds the record for home runs in the first year of an expansion team, though Dave Kingman broke the Mets record for home runs in a season in 1976 with 37 (and hit 37 again in 1982). Thomas spent three more seasons in the major leagues and played his last game for Chicago in 1966. He felt he could have continued to be productive but didn't get another legitimate chance.

"I wanted to reach 300 home runs in my career," Thomas said. "And I fell short 14. But if they would have given me the opportunity to play, I would have reached that figure."

After baseball, Thomas worked with a Pittsburgh business school and talked to local kids about the importance of education. He has eight children, 12 grandchildren and two step-grandchildren. He can still hit: "I always said, once you're a hitter, you never forget how to hit."

GENE WOODLING died June 2, 2001, in Barberton, Ohio, two months shy of his 79th birthday.

The Broadcasters

The original team of **LINDSEY NELSON, BOB MURPHY** and **RALPH KINER** broadcast every Mets game through 1978, when Nelson left to work in the Giants' radio booth. Murphy retired after calling the Mets' 2003 season, but Kiner planned to be on the microphone when the 2004 season opens.

Kiner was the first of the three to be inducted into the National Baseball Hall of Fame, the only player voted in by the baseball writers in 1975. Nelson was inducted into into the sportscasters' wing in 1988, and Murphy followed in 1994.

Nelson died in 1995 of complications associated with Parkinson's disease. He was 76.

The Coaches

CASEY STENGEL managed the Mets through 1965 and was inducted into the National Baseball Hall of Fame immediately after his retirement. He lived long enough to see the New York Mets win their second pennant in 1973 and died September 29, 1975, in Glendale, California.

Of Stengel's coaches, only SOLLY HEMUS is still alive. ROGERS HORNSBY and RED KRESS each died shortly after the 1962 season ended, the 55-year-old Kress in November, and Hornsby, a 66-year-old Hall of Famer, in January. RED RUFFING lived to be 80 years old, but missed the Mets' second World Championship by eight months when he died in February, 1986. COOKIE LAVAGETTO, who was a spry 50 years old during the 1962 season, lived 27 more before he died in 1990.

Solly Hemus turned 80 on April 17, 2003. He still goes in to work some afternoons at the Texas oil business he started in 1966.

A NOTE ON SOURCES

The 1962 Mets' season has been well documented, at the time by a dozen New York newspapers, and later in a number of well-written, funny, thoughtful books. The season generated quite a collection of lore, which has in turn taken on its own life, growing and changing with each retelling.

I relied heavily on accounts of the season in the *New York Times* and *Newsday*, as well as New York's other daily newspapers. I also drew on several books, most important among them: George Vecsey's *No Joy in Mudville* (McCall, 1970); Leonard Schecter's *Once Upon a Time* (Dial, 1969); Jimmy Breslin's *Can't Anybody Here Play This Game* (Viking, 1963); Leonard Koppett's *The New York Mets: The Whole Story* (Macmillan, 1970); Ralph Kiner's autobiography *Kiner's Korner* (Arbor House, 1987); Jonathan Fraser Light's amazingly comprehensive *Cultural Encyclopedia of Baseball* (McFarland, 1997). The on-line databases retrosheet.org, baseball-almanac.com, and baseball-reference.com were also invaluable in double-checking dates, scores and statistics.

These sources were immeasurably helpful. They informed my interviewing process and served to confirm players' stories and occasionally add details obscured by the passage of more than 40 years. Most of the tales in this book have been told over and over again, with seemingly endless variations. Still, the players were the best sources for this collection, and ultimately I trusted their memories above all else.